King penguins on South Georgia (Photo: Yongyut Kumsri/Shutterstock.com).

A Barbary macaque with a view of the Rock of Gibraltar to the rear (Photo: Anilah/Shutterstock.com).

BRITAIN'S DISTANT LANDS

THE UK OVERSEAS TERRITORIES

STEWART MCPHERSON

REDFERN NATURAL HISTORY PRODUCTIONS

Redfern Natural History Productions
Poole, Dorset, England
www.redfernnaturalhistory.com

Britain's Distant Lands: the UK Overseas Territories
ISBN 978-1-908787-31-6

Copyright © Stewart McPherson

Edited by Alastair Robinson

All rights reserved. First printed December, 2018
Printed in India by Replika Press Pvt Ltd

REDFERN NATURAL HISTORY
PRODUCTIONS LIMITED

SPECIAL THANKS TO

the Don Hanson Charitable Foundation
and the Friends of the British Overseas Territories

Working together to provide knowledge and inspire awareness about nature, science and the conservation of our world.

One copy of this book has been donated to each of 10,000 primary schools across the United Kingdom and her Overseas Territories.

WWW.DONHANSONCHARITABLEFOUNDATION.ORG   WWW.FOTBOT.ORG

A black browed albatross mating pair (Photo: Renee Vititoe/Shutterstock.com).

Contents

ACKNOWLEDGMENTS

I would like to take this opportunity to sincerely thank all those individuals and organisations in the UK Overseas Territories and their administrations for allowing me and my team to visit, making us feel welcome, and helping me to document the wildlife, history and heritage of the UK Overseas Territories. Your advice and help finding, studying, photographing and filming the animals, plants and other subjects featured in this work was essential.

I would like to express my sincere thanks to the following individuals: Sarah-Louise Adams, Samantha Addison, Andrew Avery, Badir Awe, Robert Azopardi, Anita Bagshaw, Jeremy Bagshaw, Laura Bambini, Andrea Barlow, Chris Bates, the late George Benjamin, Keith Bensusan, Arlette Betts, Jane Bevan, the late Lois Blumenthal, Jenny Bonner, Sam Breit, Alissa Breit, Robert Breit, Paul Brewin, Paul Brickle, Dave Brown, Lea Brown, Sarah Browning, Margaret Buchanan, Henry Burgess, Sean Burns, Fred Burton, Rebecca Cairns-Wicks, Sukey Cameron, Mark Capes, Chris Carnegy, Peter Carr, Devon Carter, Lucy Ceasar, Nikki Chapman, Pantelis Charilou, Emily Christian, Jacqui Christian, the late Julie Christian, Michele Christian, Nadine Christian, Randy Christian, Shawn Christian, Steve Christian, Darren Christie, Michael Clarke, Paul Cole, Julie Coleman, Martin Collins, Rupert Compston, Rhon Connor, Paul Cook, Lorna Cook, Alison Copeland, John Cortes, Mat Cottam, Clive Crisp, Sarah Crofts, Keino Daley, James 'Scriber' Daley, Andrew Darlow, Michael Dean, James Dong, David Doxford, Eddie Duff, Darren Duncan, Jonathan Eames, Gina Ebanks-Petrie, Jacqui Ellick, Sue Pole Evans, David Pole Evans, Melva Evans, Darren Fa, Wesley Fairhall, Tessa Feeney, James Fenton, Calvin Fenton, Eudora Fergus, Nicholas Ferrary, Stewart Finlayson, Geraldine Finlayson, Clive Finlayson, Anthony Flemming, Chris Flook, Eleanor Floyd, Nathan Fowler, Derren Fox, Sarita Francis, Keiron Fraser, Julia Frater, Charles Frater, Geoff Fridjohn, Herbert Ford, Deirdre Galbraith, Janine Galliano, Kevin George, Camille Gerald, Ethlyn Gibbs-Williams, Trevor Glass, James Glass, Conrad Glass, Brendan Godley, Brian Gomila, Dylan Gomila, Emily Goodnight, Mauvis Gore, Gerard Gray, Harold Green, Cynthia Green, Anne Green, Amy Green, Darralyn Griffiths, Richard Grundy, Thomas Hadjikriakou, Jeremy Harris, Guy Harvey, Helen Havercroft, Jim Hellemn, Katrine Herian, Katrine Herian, Chris Hillman, Karim Hodge, Kenneth Hodge, Oliver Hodge, Jeremy Holden, Marc Holland, Rachel Holland, Tyson Lee Holmes, Rohan Holt, Dane Hunter, Robert Irving, Leslie Jaques, Lianna Jarecki, Bradley Johnson, Matt Jolly, Geoff Jones, Sean Kerby, Jim Kerr, Mohamed Kudu, Phil Lambdon, Holly Latham, David Lea, Jennifer Lee, Deni Leo, Catherine Leo, Eric Lew, Leslie Linares, Julie Lipski, Clarissa Lloyd, Sarah Lurcock, Jenny Luxton, Jeremy Madeiros, Stuart Mailer, Lourens Malan, Bryan Naqqi Manco, Guy Marot, John Marotta, Ronald Lewis-Smith, Lloyd Martin, Stephen Massam, Ronald Massicott, Trevor Mayellan, Paul McCarthy, Croy McCoy, Rob McGill, Richard McKee, Richard McKee, Eric McKenzie, Gavin McLeod, Stephen Mendes, Heather Menzies, Jason Mesilio, Jodie Mills, Vincent Minda, Hasene Mitham, Alex Mitham, Tom Moody, Leigh Morris, Farah Mukhida, Deloris Mullings, Philemon 'Mappie' Murrain, Keith Neale, Alison Neil, Karl Netto, Paul Newbegin, William Ng, Sue O'Keefe, Edwina O'Mahoney, Henry Odbert, Steffen Oppel, Rupert Ormond, Janice Panton, Nancy Woodfield Pascoe, Andi Pearl, Tara Pelembe, Susannah Penn, Alexia Perdiou, Charlie Perez, Robert Peters, Isabel Peters, Andrew Pettit, Colville Petty, Jean Pierre, Christina McTaggart Pineda, Wallace Platts, Albert Poggio, Jérôme Poncet, Dion Poncet, Kobus Potgieter, Brian Quinn, Achut Reddy, Nick Rendell, Mike Rendell, David Renolds, Paul Repetto, Lorraine Repetto, Dawn Repetto, Gary Repetto, Geraldine Repetto, Julian Repetto, Peter Richardson, Janeczka Richardson, Lorena Rivas, Vincent Robba, Peter Roberts, Leona Roberts, Philippe Rouja, Eric Salamanca, Calvin Samuel, Andre Samuel, Amdeep Sanghera, Ben Sansom, Patricia Saxton, George Schellenger, Helen Scott, Sue Scott, Brice Semmens, Eric Shaw, Philip Shearer, Eyleen Shell, Charles Sheppard, Anne Sheppard, Marlene Short, Jolene Sim, Rhondi Skelton, Jon Slayer, Sandra Smith, Simon Smith, Roy Smith, Jimmy Smith, Joseph Smith Abbott, David Spivack, Julia Springett, Lucinda Spurling, Kathy Squires, Helen Stevens, Jon Stone, David M. Stone, Georgina Strange, Ian Strange, Stedson Stroud, Andy Summers, George Swain, Neil Swain, Joan Thomas, Vanessa Thomas, Nick Thorpe, Mike Thorpe, Edward Thorpe, Liesl Torres, Allan Trow, Mike Vallee, Neil van Niekerk, Todd van Sickle, Kathy van Zyl, Lynda Varlack, Dennis Varouxis, Juliet Vickery, Kristina Vincent, Dane Wade, Janine Wade, Ian Walker, Stephen Warr, Carol Warren, Jay Warren, Mavis Warren, Meralda Warren, Mike Warren, Nola Warren, Pawl Warren, Reynold Warren, Danielle Watler, Paul Watler, Sam Weber, Nicola Weber, Paul Welbourn, Colin Wells, Jean White, Natasha Williams, Aurjul Wilson, Henry Wilson, Dominque Witter, Kedell Worboys, Peter Young, Simon Young, Shirley Young, Kerry Young, Brian Young, Kari Young.

I would like to express my deep gratitude to the following organisations: the Government of Anguilla, Anguilla National Trust, Department of Fisheries, Marine Resources, Anguilla Heritage Collection Museum, the Anguilla Archaeological, Historical Society; the Government of Ascension Island, Ascension Island Conservation Department, Ascension Heritage Society, Ascension Island Museum and the Royal Air Force; the Government of Bermuda, Bermuda National Trust, Bermuda Department of Conservation Services, the Bermuda Aquarium, Museum, Zoo; the British Indian Ocean Territory Administration, the crew of the *Ithubaaru 3*, Blue n White Production Coordinators; the Government of the Cayman Islands, Cayman Islands Department of Environment, National Trust for the Cayman Islands, Blue Iguana Recovery Program, the Grouper Moon Project; the Government of the Falkland Islands, Falklands Conservation, Falkland Islands Museum, National Trust, New Island Conservation Trust, Wildlife Conservation Society, the Falkland Islands Fisheries Department; the Government of Gibraltar, Gibraltar Ornithological, Natural History Society, the Gibraltar Museum; the Government of Montserrat, Montserrat National Trust, Department of Environment, the Montserrat Volcano Observatory; the Government of the Pitcairn Islands, Pitcairn Island Council, Pitcairn Island Museum, the crew of the *Claymore II*, the Pitcairn Islands Study Centre; the Polar Regions Department of the Foreign, Commonwealth Office; the Government of Saint Helena, Saint Helena Environment Management Department, Nature Resources Department of Saint Helena, Saint Helena National Trust, the Wirebird Team, Saint Helena Museum, Andrew Weir Shipping Ltd, the staff of the RMS *Saint Helena*; the Government of South Georgia, the South Sandwich Islands, South Georgia Heritage Trust, the crews of the *Hans Hansson* and *Golden Fleece*; the Sovereign Base Area Administration in Cyprus, the Royal Air Force, the Akrotiri Environmental Education Centre; the Government of Tristan da Cunha, Tristan da Cunha Island Council, Tristan da Cunha Conservation Department, Tristan da Cunha Fisheries, Conservation Department, Arnold Halberstadt of the vessel *Supreme Lady*; the Government of the Turks, Caicos Islands, Turks, Caicos National Museum, Turks, Caicos National Trust, Department of Environment, Coastal Resources, the Turks, Caicos Islands Turtle Project team; the Government of the Virgin Islands, National Parks Trust of the Virgin Islands, Department of Environment, Fisheries, Ministry of Natural Resources, Labour, and the Jost van Dyke Preservation Society.

I am indebted to those who assisted me after my return with planning and completion of the project, including: Colin Clubbe, Martin Hamilton and Rebecca Upson of the Royal Botanic Gardens, Kew, for their advice and help in the planning of this project and for making crucial introductions on my behalf to contacts across the UK Overseas Territories. I would like to thank the following cameramen who joined me for different parts of my journey: Simon Vacher, Stuart Trowell, Jon Slayer, Rohan Holt and Richard Stevenson. It was a pleasure to travel with you all, and I thank you for your determined efforts to film and photograph throughout our visits to the Territories. I would like to express heartfelt gratitude to Mike and Ann Pienkowski and Catherine Wensink of the UK Overseas Territories Conservation Forum for all of their help in the completion of this book. In particular, thank you Mike and Alastair Robinson for your editing work and the countless enhancements which you so kindly put forward. To those who contributed images to this work, thank you so much for your photographs. From the outset, I hoped to show the incredible of biodiversity of all the UK Overseas Territories to a wide audience, and your kind contributions have allowed this dream to come true. All photograph contributors are credited in the image captions.

I am grateful for the assistance of the many organisations who have helped this project in other ways, including: the Amphibian and Reptile Conservation Trust, Army Ornithological Society, Bedales School, Blue Marine Foundation, Buglife, Chagos Conservation Trust, Darwin Initiative, Don Hanson Charitable Trust; Durrell Wildlife Conservation Trust, Falklands Conservation, Flora and Fauna International, Friends of the British Overseas Territories, Guy Harvey Ocean Foundation, Helping Hand, International Union for Conservation of Nature, International Union for Conservation of Nature National Committee for the UK, Joint Nature Conservation Committee, Marine Conservation Society, People's Trust for Endangered Species, Pew Charitable Trusts, Reef Environmental Education Foundation, Rotary Foundation, Rotary club of Poole (Rotary district 1110), Royal Air Force Ornithological Society, Royal Botanic Gardens Kew, Royal Society for the Protection of Birds, Shallow Marine Surveys Group (Falkland Islands), South Georgia Heritage Trust, Southern Cross Club, the UK Overseas Territories Association and the UK Overseas Territories Conservation Forum.

I would like to thank the Foreign and Commonwealth Office for allowing my visit to the British Indian Ocean Territory, completing my journey. I would like to thank Kylie Bamford, Lara Klopper, Eram Qureshi-Hasan and all FCO representatives relating to the UK Overseas Territories for the kind assistance that they have extended to me, and sincere thanks to Ben Merrick for reviewing this work. I also thank the Royal Air Force for transport to and from Ascension Island and the Falklands, and the team at RAF Brize Norton for allowing me to film and photograph the start of my journey despite their very busy schedules!

Lastly, a very sincere thank you to all at the Don Hanson Charitable Foundation and the Friends of the British Overseas Territories for making possible the donation of one copy of this book to each of 10,000 primary schools across the UK and her Overseas Territories. I extend my particular thanks to Andrew Fox, Simon Leary and Philip Smith for making the publication of this title possible.

Stewart McPherson

King penguin chicks and adults on Salisbury Plain, on South Georgia (Photo: Shutterstock / Tim Greyhavens)

INTRODUCTION

The UK Overseas Territories collectively total an area that is seven times the size of the mainland United Kingdom. The territories grant the UK the 5th largest ocean jurisdiction (6 732 963 sq. km) in the world and the 12th largest area of coral reefs (5500 sq. km). The territories also make the UK the only nation in the world to have sovereign land in all seven major oceans and seas, namely the North Atlantic, South Atlantic, Southern Ocean, Caribbean Sea, Mediterranean Sea, and the Indian and Pacific Oceans.

The territories support every one of Earth's major ecosystems: rainforests, temperate heathlands, reefs, mangrove forests, polar tundra, icy wastes, tropical dry forests, savannah scrub and barren deserts. Their landscapes include active volcanoes, salt lagoons, atolls, glaciers and ice sheets. This bewildering habitat diversity supports over 20 times the number of species found in the British Isles, including at least 1000 animals and plants that exist nowhere else on Earth. Many of the UK Overseas Territories include wilderness areas which represent some of the last remaining large-scale pristine tracts in our world. Millions of migratory seabirds, marine mammals and sea turtles are drawn to hundreds of key refuge sites across the territories to rear their young. The biggest of these breeding colonies represent some of the greatest concentrations of animals found anywhere on Earth; many are essential to the survival of wildlife ecosystems that span entire hemispheres.

Approximately 270 000 people also call the UK Overseas Territories home. Most are British subjects and some live on the most remote inhabited islands in the world. Every territory has a rich and varied history that is often surprisingly entwined with the UK's colonial past, as well as with many of the major global events of past centuries. Despite these extraordinary attributes, very few Britons know that the UK Overseas Territories exist, or that they form part of the United Kingdom today. Even fewer appreciate the Territories' full range of natural, historical and cultural treasures.

It is this treasure—this secret heritage of the United Kingdom—that is showcased in this book. These territories and their remarkable wildlife have received surprisingly little coverage in literature, notable exceptions being the book 'Outposts' by Simon Winchester (1985), which recounts a journey to ten of the current Overseas Territories, and 'The Teatime Islands' by Ben Fogle (2003), which covers six territories in enjoyable travelogues detailing the personal experiences of the respective authors. Even more inspiring is a more academic title, 'Fragments of Paradise' by Sara Oldfield (1987), which underscores the responsibility of the UK—under international agreements—to safeguard the territories, and provides an inventory of many of the key animal and plant species found in thirteen of the UK Overseas Territories. These include exotic species that one might scarcely believe were the UK Government's responsibility to protect and conserve: iguanas, penguins, giant land crabs, cacti, seals and tortoises are just some of the organisms listed amongst the book's chapters.

This book is the result of personal visits made by the author to all of the UK Overseas Territories to document as much of their wildlife, history and cultural heritage as possible, and thereby raise awareness of these incredible places. The long journey to visit each of the territories began on 15 February 2012 and took four years to complete, resulting in a natural history documentary series, Britain's Treasure Islands, that was broadcast on the BBC (UK), National Geographic (USA) and SBS (Australia). It also gave rise to a large companion book by the same title, as well as 42 online, free-to-view mini documentaries (www.britainstreasureislands.com) that document and showcase the wildlife, history and cultures of the Overseas Territories.

This book provides an overview of all of the UK Overseas Territories along with specially drawn maps that illustrate the territories and their significant landmarks. Each of the 14 territories is addressed separately in its own chapter, which provides an overview of the history, landscapes, people and wildlife of that territory, with content varied to emphasise the subjects that are of particular importance within the context of particular territories.

Great fig trees at the top of Green Mountain, Ascension Island (Photo: Stewart McPherson).

The UK Overseas Territories

The UK Overseas Territories are territories that remain under the jurisdiction and sovereignty of the United Kingdom. The history of these territories is inseparable from the story of the British Empire. Britain dominated the world commercially, industrially and militarily for centuries; over the course of four hundred years, she built the largest empire the world has ever seen. At its peak, the British Empire encompassed one-fifth of the world's population and almost one-quarter of the Earth's total land area. However the two World Wars brought the United Kingdom to her knees. The price of defending world freedom and liberating millions from tyrannical forces amounted to more wealth than Britain had accumulated during the previous century. Emerging into the light of victory in 1945, it was clear that the UK could no longer afford to maintain an empire, nor—after fighting Nazi oppression for six long years—was imperial power still regarded as either morally justifiable or desirable.

The post-war decades saw Britain and other European powers shed their colonies across the globe, giving the promise of hope and an independent future to hundreds of millions of people. The transfer of the sovereignty of Hong Kong to the People's Republic of China on 1 July 1997 marked the end of the British Empire and a new chapter in world history. During the 50 year decolonisation process, several British colonial possessions elected to remain under the sovereignty of the United Kingdom rather than become fully independent states. The British Nationality Act of 1981 redefined most of these lands as British Dependent Territories, but the word 'dependent' was a poor reflection of their voluntary association with the United Kingdom. The British Overseas Territories Act of 2002 offered a new name, and with this, the UK Overseas Territories (UKOTs) were officially born. Today, there are officially 14 UK Overseas Territories scattered across the world:

- North Atlantic Ocean: (1) Bermuda and (2) Turks and Caicos Islands.
- South Atlantic Ocean: (3) Falkland Islands, (4) Saint Helena, Ascension and Tristan da Cunha, (5) South Georgia and the South Sandwich Islands.
- Southern Ocean: (6) British Antarctic Territory.
- Indian Ocean: (7) British Indian Ocean Territory.
- Pacific Ocean: (8) Pitcairn Islands.
- Caribbean Sea: (9) Anguilla, (10) British Virgin Islands, (11) Cayman Islands, (12) Montserrat.
- Mediterranean Sea: (13) Gibraltar, (14) Sovereign Base Areas of Akrotiri and Dhekelia.

Bermuda and the Turks and Caicos Islands are usually grouped with the four Caribbean Territories (the British West Indies) due to their strong ecological, historic and cultural ties, even though they are located in the North Atlantic. Saint Helena, Ascension and Tristan da Cunha collectively comprise one UK Overseas Territory, but these three groups of islands are so isolated and ecologically different from each another that they are featured separately in this work. The British Antarctic Territory and South Georgia and the South Sandwich Islands do not have permanent populations, just visiting scientific teams. Ascension Island and Akrotiri and Dhekelia are military bases, but they also house civilian populations of varying degrees of permanence, but the civilians of the latter are mostly citizens of the Republic of Cyprus. The British Indian Ocean Territory does not have a resident civilian population.

World Map with the UK Overseas Territories Indicated

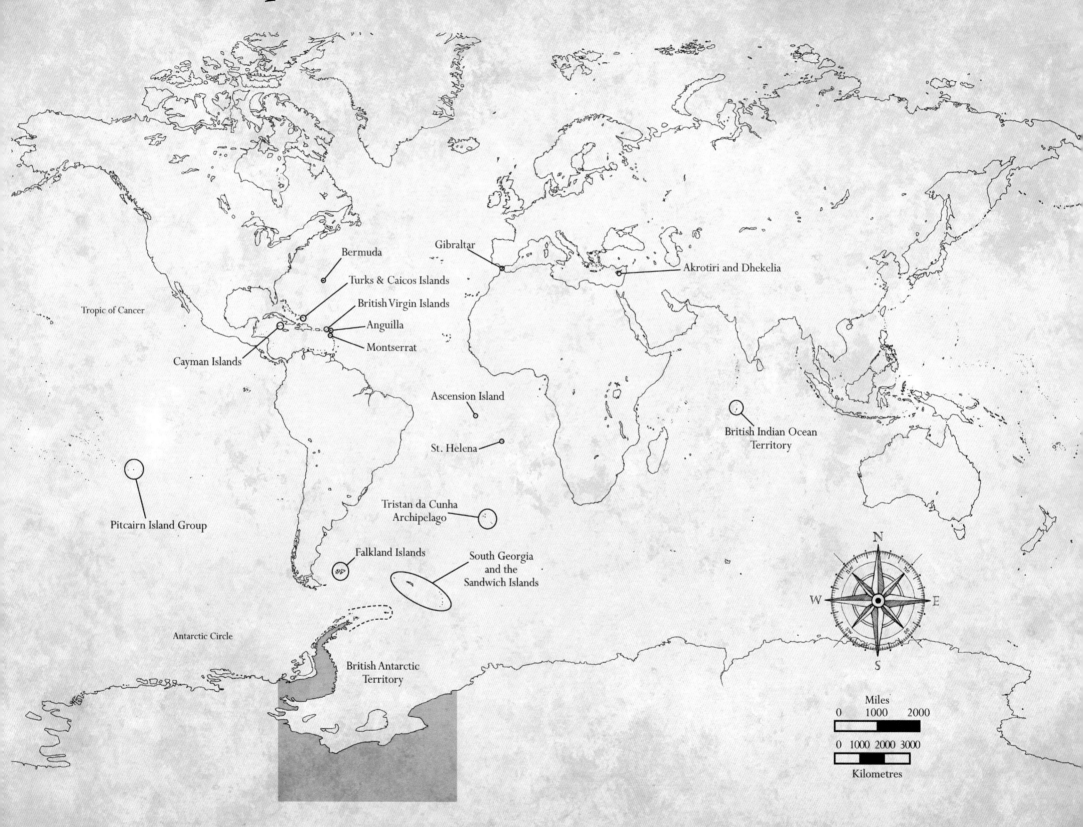

Bermuda

Turks & Caicos Islands

British Virgin Islands

Anguilla

Montserrat

Gibraltar

Akrotiri and Dhekelia

Tropic of Cancer

Cayman Islands

Ascension Island

British Indian Ocean Territory

St. Helena

Pitcairn Island Group

Tristan da Cunha Archipelago

Falkland Islands

South Georgia and the Sandwich Islands

Antarctic Circle

British Antarctic Territory

N

W   E

S

Miles

0   1000   2000

0   1000 2000 3000

Kilometres

The inhabited UK Overseas Territories are largely self-governing countries. They have their own internally elected leaders, but all share the British monarch as the head of state. The UK is responsible for the defence, foreign relations and governance of all of the territories, but internal rule is the responsibility of each territory's Assembly and Government. The precise degree of direct responsibility delegated by the UK to elected officials and retained by the Governor or Administrator (both UK officials) varies between territories and, in some places, has changed over time.

The status of the UK Overseas Territories is not widely understood in the United Kingdom, let alone elsewhere. Senior British politicians, Lords and Members of Parliament frequently refer to the Overseas Territories as colonies, usually inadvertently, but sometimes also treat them as independent states without any political association with the UK. Unfortunately, many journalists do the same, sometimes to sensationalise or politicise their articles. This is particularly the case abroad and is especially the case when discussing the Falkland Islands and Gibraltar. Against the wishes of their populations, many of the UK Overseas Territories remain listed by the United Nation's Special Committee on Decolonisation, even though independence has been democratically rejected, in some cases repeatedly and near-unanimously. The Overseas Territories are united with the UK in opposing critics who disregard the right of the territories' electorates to self-determination and their right to remain connected to the UK if that is what their electorates choose.

The relationship between the UK and the Overseas Territories may seem complex, though in reality it is not. The United Kingdom of Great Britain and Northern Island is a sovereign state. England, Northern Ireland, Scotland and Wales are all countries within the UK. Each of the territories is also a country under UK sovereignty. The people of each Overseas Territory are subjects of Britain, as well as of their respective territory. For example, the citizens of Gibraltar are both Gibraltarian and British subjects, whereas a person born in London is both English and British because they were born in England.

All the citizens of the territories, except those of Akrotiri and Dhekelia, are entitled to British citizenship and have the right to live in the United Kingdom. However, the citizens of the territories do not have the automatic right to live or work in any of the other UK Overseas Territories. Similarly, citizens of England, Northern Ireland, Scotland and Wales do not have an automatic right to live or work in any of the Overseas Territories.

Even though all the citizens of the Overseas Territories are British subjects, each Territory has its own unique culture, customs and laws. All the Territories speak English, although many have distinct accents, and Gibraltar and Pitcairn have unique dialect-languages that can sound surprisingly unfamiliar to non-speakers. Many have their own currencies and unique ways of life, but drive on the left-hand side of the road, except in the British Indian Ocean Territory and Gibraltar.

The UK Overseas Territories choose to remain under UK sovereignty for a number of different reasons. The status of Overseas Territory offers the following advantages: protection in case of foreign invasion (e.g. the Falkland Islands); direct assistance and a place to evacuate to in the event of catastrophic emergency (e.g. Montserrat and Tristan da Cunha); access to external funding, but perhaps more importantly, the guarantee of financial responsibility and security by one of the largest economies in the world; varying degrees of access to the markets of the UK's trading partners; international travel on the same terms as UK citizens; health care via the NHS in the UK; and the maintenance of identities and cultural ties that have been built up over centuries.

Several of the Overseas Territories are home to the most remote permanent settlements on Earth. A few are among the wealthiest countries in the world, with per capita GDP levels far higher than those of England, Northern Ireland, Scotland or Wales. While some Overseas Territories do require occasional support from the UK, such as following natural disasters, most are economically self-sufficient and do not receive any financial support from the UK.

The future of the UK Overseas Territories lies in the hands of the citizens of each territory. The British Government encourages the elected representatives of each territory to uphold the democratic wishes of the people they represent, and maintains a clear long-term position: that the non-military/inhabited Overseas Territories may remain under UK sovereignty for so long as their citizens wish. Indeed, many of the UK Overseas Territories have been British for longer than the United States have been American; who else but the people of these lands should have the right to decide their own futures?

The volcanic landscape of Ascension island (Photo: Simon Vacher).

Population: 806 (2016)
Area: 87 sq. km of dry land
Currency: Saint Helena pound
Capital: Georgetown
Flag: A Blue Ensign bearing the Ascension Coat of Arms—two turtles supporting a shield that shows Green Mountain and three Wideawake Terns.

ASCENSION ISLAND

Located in the South Atlantic just over 1500 kilometres from the coastline of Liberia, on the African continent, Ascension Island is one of the most remote inhabited islands on Earth. Although the island was visited by a number of explorers across three centuries, including João da Nova, in 1501, and Afonso de Albuquerque in 1503—who sighted and named the island on May 21st, Ascension Day—both in service of Portugal, it was not until 1815 that the island was claimed and occupied for Britain by the Royal Navy.

Up to this point, the volcanic island had been regarded as too barren and inhospitable to be of value. However, when the deposed Emperor of the French, Napoléon Bonaparte, was exiled to the neighbouring island of Saint Helena 1285 kilometres to the southeast, Ascension was garrisoned as a precautionary measure. A garrison of the Royal Marines was also stationed on the island from 1823. When eminent naturalist Charles Darwin visited Ascension in 1836 aboard the HMS *Beagle*, he described the island as a treeless, arid place, supporting a few hundred grazing animals, as well as imported Guinea-fowl, rats, mice and land crabs, but noted that the meagre resources, particularly water, were extremely well managed, allowing for crop growth near the fern-covered summit of the highest peak on the island, and otherwise barren feature known as Green Mountain.

Green Mountain would prove to be the site of one of the greatest biological experiments of the time, and one which is still ongoing. Botanist Joseph Hooker, with encouragement from Darwin, suggested that vegetating the slopes of Green Mountain could serve to capture water from the moisture-laden oceanic winds and improve soil. This process began in 1847, with hundreds of species of plants introduced by 1860. With drought tolerant species planted lower on the mountain and moisture loving ones planted towards the summit, a sustainable planned forest was created. By 1890, reports spoke of complete vegetation of the peak and increased water supply which endures to this day. The top of the mountain boasts the world's only example of a man-made rainforest.

As the island's strategic importance increased, so grew dependence on the natural resources it did offer, among them abundant turtle meat, seabird eggs, vegetables and water, to the point that the island became a major victualling station, allowing ships to be re-stocked with meat, water and other provisions on the long journeys to the Capes of Africa and South America. It was also the base for the West Africa Squadron which, during the 1830s, enforced the British anti-slavery policy, patrolling the African coast with anti-slaving ships that sought out and liberated captives on slave vessels. In this respect this modest island shaped the development of the British Empire! The harvesting of sea turtles and birds eggs, coupled with predation by introduced rats, cats and mice, saw resources plummet to critical levels. This led to the end of turtle hunting, the eradication of cats and the creation of protective sanctuaries on the island, leading to a dramatic turnaround in the fortunes of native fauna.

Ascension Island

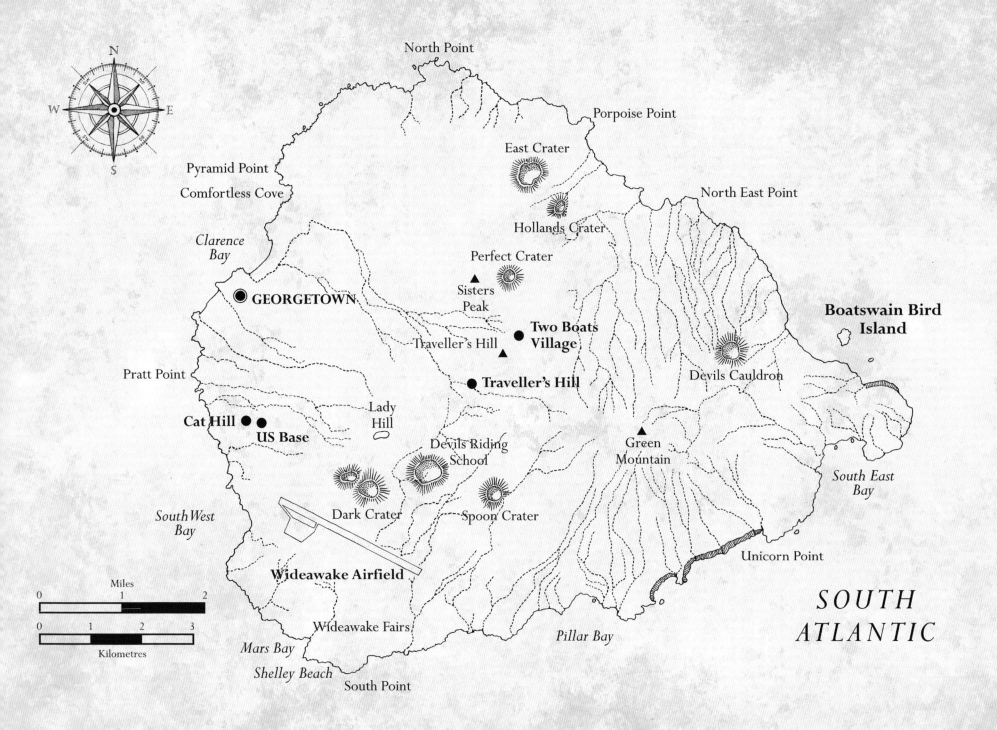

North Point

Porpoise Point

East Crater

North East Point

Pyramid Point

Comfortless Cove

Hollands Crater

Clarence
Bay

Perfect Crater

Sisters
Peak

GEORGETOWN

**Two Boats
Village**

Boatswain Bird
Island

Traveller's Hill

Pratt Point

Traveller's Hill

Devils Cauldron

Lady
Hill

Cat Hill

US Base

Devils Riding
School

Green
Mountain

South East
Bay

Dark Crater

Spoon Crater

South West
Bay

Unicorn Point

Wideawake Airfield

Wideawake Fairs

Pillar Bay

**SOUTH
ATLANTIC**

Mars Bay

Shelley Beach

South Point

Miles

0   1   2

0   1   2   3

Kilometres

Cannons overlooking Georgetown (Photo: Stewart McPherson).

Georgetown

The capital of Ascension Island is Georgetown, a town of about 450 people situated on the northwest coast of the island.

Named after the reigning monarch, King George III, the town was the chosen site of the naval base established on Ascension in 1816 to guard the island against the French. In 1830, work began on relocating the centre of Georgetown further back from the sea to an elevated plateau where conditions were better. A number of the town's major buildings, including its hospital, Old Barracks and church, St. Mary's, hail from this period.

Native 'Ascensionians' are relatively few as the people living on the island are mainly those based there for work, either as servicemen and women at the British and American military installations, or those working for the government, their contractors or broadcasting companies like the BBC.

Of course, some people have started families there, so a civilian population does exist. To this end, Georgetown boasts a school, a supermarket, a post office and a small number of cafés and restaurants that cater to the island's residents and the few tourists that arrive each year.

In addition to the historical buildings present on the island, including Georgetown's forts, attractions include great wildlife spectacles, trekking and scuba diving in the rich waters off the coast.

The Anglican church of St Mary in Georgetown (Photo: Simon Vacher).

Turtle carcasses used to supply meat (Photo: Ascension Island Heritage Society).

Scant vegetation dots the alien landscape of Ascension Island (Photo: Stewart McPherson).

Landscape and Habitats

Ascension Island is the emergent tip of a stratovolcano whose base lies 3000 metres below the sea and rises to 859 metres above sea level. The island is geologically young, having emerged from beneath the waves during an eruptive phase that occurred just one million years ago. As a result much of its landscape consists of volcanic rubble derived from basaltic lava flows, with views in many directions punctuated by its 44 craters and even more numerous lava domes, evidence of its highly active volcanic past.

Although no eruptions have occurred since at least the late 1400s, the relatively low rainfall of this sub-tropical island has left much of it barren, though its highest peaks were covered in ferns by the time the island was first described by explorers. Today, the island is increasingly green as a result of historic efforts to increase vegetation cover, particularly on Green Mountain, the site of the main volcanic vent of the island (situated below the summit at 595 m elevation).

In this respect, the island is highly unusual, having many of the characteristics of a desertic landscape, but with nearby peaks covered in cloud forest. Coupled with its extensive shoreline, which includes sandy beaches, towering sea cliffs and isolated lava rockpools, there are numerous habitats within which the endemic species of the island have been able to evolve.

A rock pool home to endemic shrimp at Shelly Beach (Photo: Stewart McPherson).

A view of Green Mountain, a source of vital water (Photo: Stewart McPherson).

A nesting female green turtle (Photo: Simon Vacher).

Egg burying (Photo: (Photo: Sam Weber, Ascension Island Government Conservation Department).

Turtles returning to the sea (Photo: Mike Pienkowski).

A turtle hatchling (Photo: Stewart McPherson).

A crab consuming a turtle egg (Photo: Stewart McPherson).

Wildlife

Although the dry, volcanic landscape of the island harbours its own endemic species, including some terrestrial invertebrates found nowhere else, it is on the coasts, cliffs, beaches and sea mounts of Ascension where much of the island's most splendid biological wealth lies. Among these are its vast populations of land crabs, many green turtles, nesting seabirds and even two species of endemic cave shrimp found in some of the island's volcanic rock pools, their nearest relatives occurring in Hawaii, Cuba and the Yucatan!

The annual number of nesting green turtles today is about 5000, versus just a few hundred by the 1860s, when rampant turtle hunting caused their numbers to crash. The island, where they are now strictly protected, is an important breeding ground for these animals, which return from their feeding grounds along the coasts of Brazil and the Caribbean to breed once they are mature.

The turtles lay their eggs in the deep sands found above the high tide mark, each female nesting up to six times per breeding season. The volcanic rocks of the island can prove problematic, occasionally trapping turtles that attempt to clamber over them on their return to the sea. To prevent their deaths, trapped turtles are rescued and returned to the sea by the local conservation team, sometimes aided by locally stationed troops.

Returning a stranded turtle to the sea (Photo: Stewart McPherson).

Land crabs gathering to release eggs (Photo: Stewart McPherson).

A species of land crab (*Johngarthia lagostoma*) is found on Ascension, foraging for vegetation and carrion close to their burrows mainly on the flanks of Green Mountain. Like other land crabs, they must return to the water to produce their young, undertaking a long overland migration from the mountain to the sea each year. Spawning events may see tens of thousands of crabs converging on the beaches to release their eggs, an amazing spectacle!

Historically, Ascension was home to some of the greatest seabird colonies on Earth. However, these were almost entirely wiped out by introduced predators, leaving vast plains of lava covered in tell-tale splotches of white: bird guano produced over the centuries and baked hard by the intense sun. Attempts to return the island to its former condition began with the eradication of cats, and though mice and rats remain a problem, this initial step has allowed rare birds like the endemic Ascension frigatebird to make an initial return to the mainland.

This remarkable bird, whose males sport a bright red gular (throat) pouch to attract mates, was rendered extinct on the Ascension mainland but managed to survive on one off-shore islet alone. With their habitat cleared of predators, conservationists were able to attract birds back to the mainland using recordings of their calls and even plastic models arranged as if they were nesting. Today, at least 200 pairs have returned to the mainland to breed.

Egg release takes place at night (Photo: Stewart McPherson).

Offshore islets are vital to the survival of some species (Photo: Simon Vacher).

A colony of masked boobies (Photo: Stewart McPherson).

The endangered Ascension Frigatebird (Photo: Stewart McPherson).

A pair of masked boobies (Photo: Jeremy Holden).

Fig trees on Green Mountain (Photo: Stewart McPherson).

Flora

Of the ten species of plant recorded as endemic to Ascension Island, only seven survive. One of the rarest of these is the parsley fern, *Anogramma ascensionis*, which was declared extinct in 2003 since no plants had been seen since 1958. However, a few individuals were located in 2010 and spores collected, allowing it to be propagated both on Ascension and at Kew Gardens.

While introduced animals like goats and rabbits have had a negative impact on native vegetation, one of the greatest threats to Ascension's plants is competition by introduced plant species. Many of these species arrived on Ascension as part of Joseph Hooker's project to vegetate Green Mountain.

Hooker, encouraged by Charles Darwin, put forward the idea of planting the summit of this central peak with trees and its slopes and valleys with shrubs and drought tolerant species. The results were remarkable; the abundant vegetation created a rudimentary soil layer with greater moisture retaining capacity, and the increased substrate moisture enabled ever greater plant communities to be sustained. Increased moisture in the ground and vegetation in turn resulted in more water evaporating, thereby increasing local air humidity, cloud cover, mist, dews and rains on the mountain.

This experiment achieved in a number of decades what usually takes hundreds or thousands of years to come about naturally.

Giant buttressed fig tree roots (Photo: Stewart McPherson).

Ferns and *Begonia* on Green Mountain (Photo: Stewart McPherson).

Marine Environment

The isolation of Ascension has spared it from intensive commercial fishing, making the island's waters amongst the most intact of all the Atlantic ecosystems, sustaining some of the word's largest marine predators including a wide variety of ocean fish like marlin and tuna but also wahoo, dorado, horse eye jacks, black jacks, amberjack, Atlantic sailfish, spearfish, oilfish, rainbow runner and dog snapper, not to mention many sharks.

Closer to shore, the island boasts at least 19 established scuba diving sites, although diving facilities remain basic given the lack of tourism infrastructure.

In 2016, the British Government announced that a 234 291 sq km marine reserve would be created in the waters around Ascension in order to protect its marine life. Amounting to an area only slightly less than the size of the United Kingdom itself, this would be the largest fully protected marine reserve in the Atlantic Ocean! However, the reserve has not yet come into being, the main obstacle facing the plan being monetary, since the selling of fishing rights to other countries has been a historically significant source of revenue for the island's economy.

The black triggerfish (*Melichthys niger*) is extremely abundant in the waters that surround Ascension Island and large shoals of this species form clouds under water (Dan Laffoley).

A reef shark off the Ascension coast (Photo: Ascension Island Government Conservation Department).

Approaching Jamestown, capital of Saint Helena (Photo: Simon Vacher).

Population: 4534 (2016)
Area: 121 sq. km of dry land
Currency: St Helena pound
Capital: Jamestown
Flag: A Blue Ensign bearing the shield from the coat of arms of Saint Helena, which depicts a plover overlooking a tall ship off the coast of the island.

SAINT HELENA

The island of Saint Helena is located in the South Atlantic 1285 kilometres to the southeast of Ascension Island and 1857 kilometres west of the coast of Angola, southern Africa. The island was first sighted in 1502 by the explorer João da Nova, travelling in the service of Portugal, during the same voyage in which he discovered Ascension. In the following years, the Portuguese introduced livestock and planted food plants in order to take advantage of the island's rich soils and abundant fresh water. However, the island was not settled by the Portuguese, nor was it settled by the Dutch who formally laid claim to the island in 1633. In fact, it was not until 1658 that the island was colonised by Britain's East India Company under charter from Oliver Cromwell, Lord Protector of the Commonwealth of England, Scotland, and Ireland following the execution of King Charles I.

The strategic location of the settlement on trade routes to India, China and southern Africa ensured that it was maintained by the East India Company, despite issues of soil erosion and drought resulting from rapid deforestation, as well as poor living conditions. As a result, successive governors made concerted efforts to replant trees across the island, in order to increase rainfall, and to improve island infrastructure, including security, food production and medical facilities. The effects of the early experiments in reforestation for environmental modification may well have inspired the efforts of Joseph Hooker to vegetate Ascension island's Green Mountain a century later. Saint Helena ceased to be administered by the East India Company following an act of parliament that saw the territory become a British crown colony in 1834.

The sheer remoteness of Saint Helena saw the island chosen as the place of exile for the Emperor of the French, Napoléon Bonaparte, in 1815. Napoléon would live on the island at his residence, Longwood House, until his death in 1821. It was also the place of exile from 1890–1897 for Dinuzulu kaCetshwayo, King of the Zulus, for resisting British annexation of their lands, as it was for over 6000 Boer prisoners of war from 1900–1902 during the Second Boer War.

The island is extremely biodiverse, with high rates of plant and animal endemism, both on land and in its surrounding waters, with over 400 endemic species recognised to date. Unfortunately the introduction of goats, rabbits, mice and invasive plant species has seen many of the island's habitats severely degraded, with overgrazing leading to the desertification of the island's once green coasts—itself leading to soil erosion and water run-off that further compound this issue—and the crowding out of native species by more aggressive foreign plants such as New Zealand flax. Efforts to combat and reverse some of this damage are being overseen by local conservationists working with foreign assistance.

Saint Helena

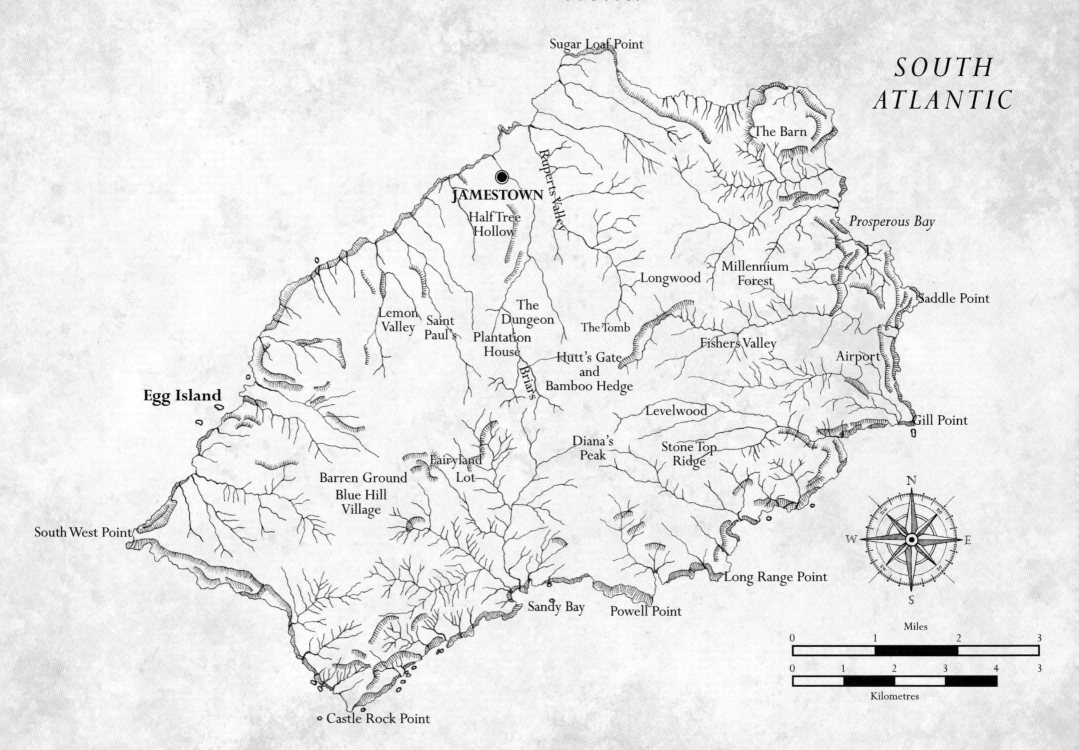

SOUTH ATLANTIC

Sugar Loaf Point

The Barn

Ruperts Valley

Prosperous Bay

JAMESTOWN

Half Tree Hollow

Millennium Forest

Longwood

Saddle Point

Lemon Valley

Saint Paul's

The Dungeon

The Tomb

Fishers Valley

Plantation House

Airport

Hutt's Gate and Bamboo Hedge

Briars

Egg Island

Levelwood

Gill Point

Diana's Peak

Stone Top Ridge

Fairyland Lot

Barren Ground Blue Hill Village

South West Point

Long Range Point

Sandy Bay

Powell Point

Castle Rock Point

Miles

0 1 2 3

0 1 2 3 4 5

Kilometres

An engraving entitled Town of St James, Island of Saint Helena, 1794 published in 1813. The island became an important victualling station.

Plantation House and its resident giant tortoise (Photo: Stewart McPherson).

Jamestown

The capital of Saint Helena is Jamestown, making it also the default capital of the British Overseas Territory of Saint Helena, Ascension and Tristan da Cunha. The settlement was named after James II of England and sits between steep cliffs in the narrow James Valley. Many of the buildings were constructed by the British East India Company during the Georgian era, with over 100 of them afforded Listed Building status.

Jamestown is officially a city, having been granted city status by Queen Victoria in 1859. Even so, it is not the largest of the 15 communities on Saint Helena, having been exceeded in population by Half Tree Hollow—initially a suburb of Jamestown—Longwood and Saint Paul's.

The economy of Jamestown and much of the island was, until 1966, dependent on the production and export of flax fibre for rope. This ended as a result of synthetic fibre production which gave rise to cheaper and stronger alternatives. As a result, the Saint Helenian economy has contracted significantly and now depends on tourism and exports of coffee and Tungi Spirit, an alcohol produced from the fruit of the prickly pear cactus.

The island's first airport was officially opened in October 2017 and is served by weekly flights from Johannesburg and Windhoek, with a monthly connection to Ascension Island, greatly increasing tourism prospects.

An 1885 depiction of Napoleon, exiled emperor of France, imprisoned on Saint Helena (Patrick Guenette/www.123rf.com).

The landscape of Saint Helena is varied and biodiverse (Photo: Stewart McPherson).

Landscape and Habitats

Believed to have once been green throughout, historic deforestation and overgrazing has left much of the coastal area of Saint Helena an arid region not dissimilar to Ascension Island. Its once green coastal areas are thus barren, while its former interior of tropical forest now remains green mainly due to the presence of introduced vegetation, including plantations, pastures and pockets of remnant vegetation.

Unlike its distant neighbour Ascension Island, Saint Helena is a more ancient volcanic landmass of approximately 14 million years of age. The last volcanic eruptions on Saint Helena are thought to have occurred about 7 million years ago. The age of the island accounts for the development of historically extensive vegetation cover, deep soils and high rates of biodiversity including significant endemism.

The island rises from the ocean to its highest point, Diana Peak, at 818 metres elevation. The peak is home to tree ferns and lush vegetation associated with cloud forest communities. The many steep cliffs, ridges, gullies and valleys of the island, as well are more than 20 offshore rocks and islet, provide ample habitat to a wide range of bird species, particularly seabirds. As a result, the island is being considered for listing as one of the United Kingdom's UNESCO World Heritage Sites.

The arid coastline of Saint Helena (Photo: Simon Vacher).

The endemic gumwood trees are actually part of the humble daisy family (Photo: Stewart McPherson).

A spiky yellow woodlouse (*Pseudolaureola atlantica*) in its normal posture (Ed Thorpe). Inset: The endemic spiky yellow woodlouse rolled into a ball in defence mode (Mike Pienkowski).

The caterpillar of *Scopula separata* (Philip Ashmole).

The endemic Shadowy Chafor (*Mellissius adumbratus*). The larv of this species are known on Saint Helena as 'hogworms' (Da Pryce).

The endemic Loveridge's hoverfly (*Sphaerophoria beattiei*) on the flower of the endemic large bellflower (*Wahlenbergia linifolia*) (Roger Key).

Another endemic woodlouse (*Littorophiloscia alticola*) (Roger Ke

The unique golden sail spider (*Argyrodes mellissi*). Note this species' shiny abdomen (Mike Thorpe).

Lelup's darkling beetle (*Tarphiophasis leleupi*) (Roger Key).

The endemic moth *Helenoscoparia scintillulalis* (Liza Fowler).

A golden sail spider and her egg sack dangling on the underside of a leaf (Photo: Stewart McPherson).

Wildlife

Although a relatively young island in geological terms, the highly isolated nature of Saint Helena has driven the evolution of the various organisms that colonised the island down unique paths. Levels of endemism are thus high among its plants, invertebrates, fungi and lichens, and moderately high amongst its birds, whilst native mammals and reptiles are entirely absent.

In the absence of their usual predators, invertebrate life on the island became particularly exuberant. For example the now extinct Saint Helena giant earwig (*Labidura herculeana*), the largest earwig ever known, reached over 8 cm in length, while the predatory giant ground beetle (*Aplothorax burchelli*) reached nearly 4 cm in length. The humble woodlouse also reached the island, giving rise to perhaps the most beautiful extant species on the island, the spiky yellow woodlouse (*Pseudolaureola atlantica*) which lives beneath the leaves of endangered endemic ferns. The island is also home to the spectacular golden sail spider (*Argyrodes mellissi*), which has a triangular, sail-shaped abdomen that is metallic gold!

These are just a few examples of the 460 endemic invertebrates that evolved on Saint Helena alongside at least 90 other native but non-endemic invertebrate species. In fact, more than fifty times the number of endemic invertebrates occur here than in the entire British Isles!

Bartlett's Bush Cricket (*Phaneracra bartleti*) (Liza Fowler).

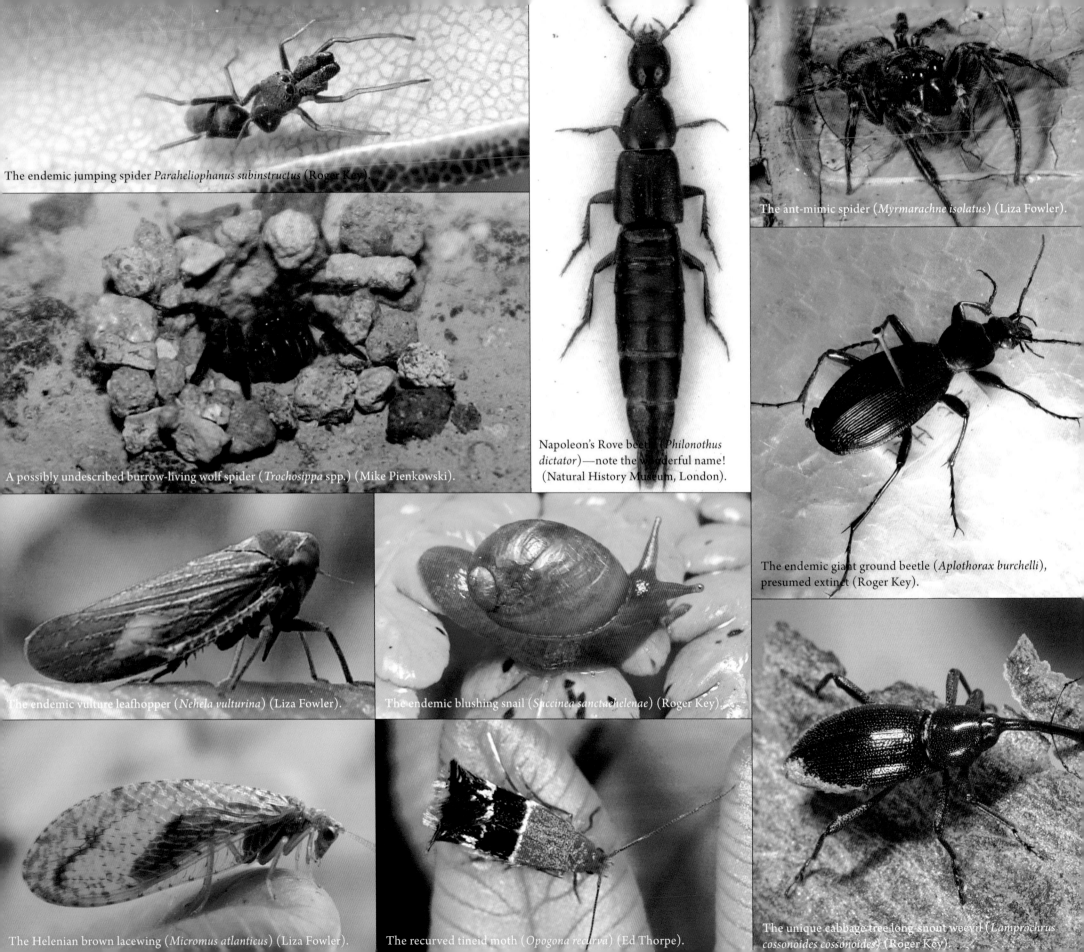

The endemic jumping spider *Paraheliophanus subinstructus* (Roger Key)

A possibly undescribed burrow-living wolf spider (*Trochosippa* spp.) (Mike Pienkowski).

The ant-mimic spider (*Myrmarachne isolatus*) (Liza Fowler).

Napoleon's Rove beetle (*Philonothus dictator*)—note the wonderful name! (Natural History Museum, London).

The endemic giant ground beetle (*Aplothorax burchelli*), presumed extinct (Roger Key).

The endemic vulture leafhopper (*Nehela vulturina*) (Liza Fowler).

The endemic blushing snail (*Succinea sanctaehelenae*) (Roger Key).

The Helenian brown lacewing (*Micromus atlanticus*) (Liza Fowler).

The recurved tineid moth (*Opogona recurva*) (Ed Thorpe).

The unique cabbage-tree long-snout weevil (*Lamprochrus cossonoides cossonoides*) (Roger Key).

Saint Helena is also home to 68 species of birds. In the recent past, the island harboured at least six endemic land bird species and three endemic seabirds. These species were all present on the island when Europeans first landed, but all but one have slipped silently into extinction in the 500 years that have elapsed since then.

The sole surviving bird is the wirebird, also known as the Saint Helena plover (*Charadrius sanctaehelenae*), the official symbol of the island. The wirebird is so-named for its thin legs. It is a small wader whose closest relatives are in sub-Saharan Africa. Tending to favour open clearings, the clearance of the once extensive woodlands across the island may have offered the wirebird considerably more viable habitat to occupy than was originally present on the island.

Censuses carried out in the 1980s and 1990s showed that numbers of this species were nonetheless in swift decline, with a low of 340 adult birds in 1998. Feral cats were identified as the main cause of this decline, leading to the initiation of a predator-control programme that saw any cats hunting near the wirebirds' breeding areas trapped and humanely euthanised.

This suppression of the predator population proved successful and the wirebird population rose to over 500 individuals by 2013, demonstrating the value of predator eradication in areas to which they are non-native.

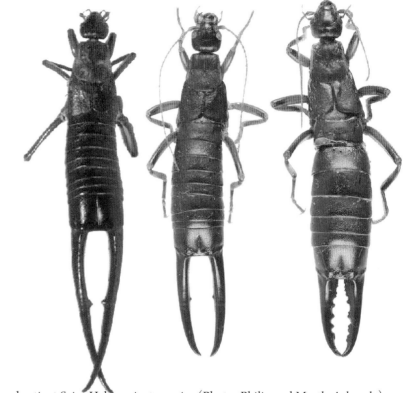

Pinned extinct Saint Helena giant earwigs (Photo: Philip and Myrtle Ashmole).

Saint Helena wirebird with young (Photo: Stewart McPherson).

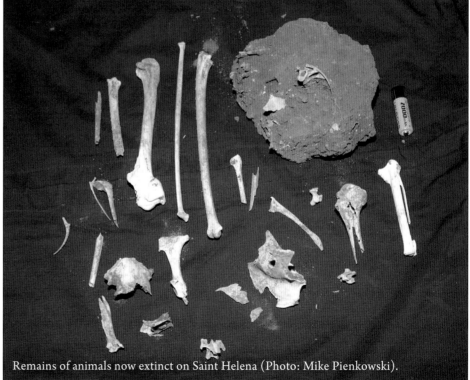

Remains of animals now extinct on Saint Helena (Photo: Mike Pienkowski).

Flowers of endemic gumwood trees (Photo: Stewart McPherson).

Flora

The dense, tropical forests which dominated the interior of Saint Helena when Europeans first landed included many remarkable plants, including the cabbage tree (*Melanodendron integrifolium*), she-cabbage tree (*Lachanodes arborea*) and gumwood (*Commidendrum* species), all of which—in an example of evolution gone wild—are in the same family as the humble and diminutive daisy!

Competition by introduced plants like New Zealand flax, the cutting down of trees for building and for fuel, as well as heavy grazing by goats decimated these forests to the end that none remain, with only patches of native trees in certain locations. Species like the bastard gumwood (*Commidendrum rotundifolium*) were reduced to just two specimens in the wild! Fortunately, their plight was recognised and the trees protected from pests and grazing animals. Careful artificial pollination resulted in great quantities of seed being produced, and their numbers have rebounded.

While great projects like the Millennium Forest have seen over 10 000 native trees raised and planted out across selected sites on the island, this important work has come too late for some species, including the string tree (*Acalypha rubrinervis*), which went extinct in about 1860, and the Saint Helena olive (*Nesiota elliptica*), which went extinct in 2003.

Replanted endemic species in the Millennium Forest (Photo: Stewart McPherson).

The extinct Saint Helena olive (Photo: Rebecca Cairns Wicks).

Marine Environment

The remoteness of Saint Helena has ensured that its marine environment is relatively unspoiled. The coast of the mainland and its offshore islands are home to 8 species of seabirds, including Madeiran storm petrels and masked boobies, while the waters surrounding the island are rich in pelagic (ocean going) fish.

Among these are majestic whale sharks—the world's largest fish species—which migrate through the region between January and April, as well as ocean going species like tuna, wahoo, marlin, dorado, devil rays and various other species of shark.

Cetaceans are also numerous, with pods of dolphins containing as many as 600 individuals regularly appearing around the island, while humpback whales make an annual appearance between June and December each year.

Close to the shore, diving opportunities abound, with a number of shipwrecks, artificial reefs and natural reefs present off the coast, all easily accessible from Jamestown on boats operated by a local diving company. At this time, the island is too remote to have developed as a significant diving destination, however with the advent of the new airport, it is possible that this may change in the near future.

A red Atlantic reef lobster (*Enoplometopus antillensis*) that has made home under a rock ledge in Saint Helena's waters (Photo: Leigh Morris)

Whale sharks (*Rhincodon typus*) are the largest fish species alive today, and frequently swim through Saint Helena's waters (Photo: Leigh Morris).

A shoal of Saint Helena butterflyfish (*Chaetodon sanctaehelenae*). This species is known only from the waters of Ascension Island and Saint Helena (Photo: Leigh Morris).

A view of Tristan da Cunha looking south west across the island (www.tristandc.com, Tristan Photo Portfolio/Royal Navy)

Population: 259 (2017)
Area: 207 sq. km of dry land, 98 sq. km on the main island
Currency: British pound
Capital: Edinburgh of the Seven Seas
Flag: A Blue Ensign bearing the Tristan coat of arms—a longboat, a naval crown, a pair of rock lobsters and four albatrosses

TRISTAN DA CUNHA

The Tristan da Cunha archipelago includes the islands of Tristan da Cunha, Gough, Inaccessible and Nightingale Islands. Tristan da Cunha is the most remote inhabited place on Earth, situated in extreme isolation in the South Atlantic an astounding 2424 kilometres from the island of Saint Helena and 2772 kilometres from Cape Town, which represents both the nearest city and the nearest continental landmass, lying on the southern tip of Africa. With no airport, visiting the island requires travel by ship or sailboat, the fastest scheduled journey taking 5 days each way.

The islands were first documented in 1506 by Tristão da Cunha, a Portuguese explorer who named the main island after himself. They were visited on a number of occasions thereafter by the Portuguese, the Dutch and the French, who mainly sheltered in the lee of the islands to repair and recover from the battering conditions of the South Atlantic. Increasing numbers of mariners also landed ashore for varying periods in search of seabird and seal meat, seal fur, eggs and fresh water, but the islands remained uninhabited until 1810 when the first permanent settlers arrived in the form of three American men, soon joined by a fourth. Three of the four died by drowning in 1812. In 1816, the islands were formally annexed by the British government as dependencies of the Cape Colonies, partly to ensure that the islands were not used to stage a rescue of French Emperor Napoléon I from his exile on Saint Helena.

As part of this annexation, a garrison was stationed on the island, but recognising that the island was too remote to be relied upon as part of any rescue attempt, the British Admiralty withdrew the garrison in November of 1817. One of the garrison's corporals, William Glass, along with his wife, two children and a pair of masons, requested that they be left behind, leading to the establishment of the present settlement. In time migrants from Saint Helena, South Africa, the Netherlands and Italy would join them.

To this day, the principles that govern life in the island's capital and only village, Edinburgh of the Seven Seas, locally called "The Settlement", are essentially those set out by Glass himself. The Settlement is based on a life of equality, with all land communally owned and each of the households afforded plots of land on which they grow potatoes. The families, who are all farmers and fishermen, maintain their own herds of cattle and sheep, but livestock numbers are strictly limited to ensure that no one family accumulates significantly greater wealth than others. All members of the community, from young to old, are involved in day to day running of the community, including farming and administrative work. During the limited fishing season, many of the farmers take to the boats to ensure a fruitful catch in the few days of good weather available to them.

Tristan da Cunha

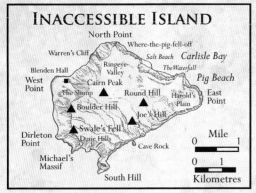

INACCESSIBLE ISLAND

North Point
Where-the-pig-fell-off
Warren's Cliff
Salt Beach
Carlisle Bay
Ringeye Valley
The Waterfall
Blenden Hall
Pig Beach
West Point
Cairn Peak
The Slump
Round Hill
Harold's Plain
East Point
Boulder Hill
Joe's Hill
Dirleton Point
Swale's Fell
Dune Hills
Cave Rock
Michael's Massif
South Hill

0   Mile   1

0   1
Kilometres

Stoltenhoff Island
Alex or Middle Island
West Landing

NIGHTINGALE ISLAND

Pequena Point
Ned's Cave
Seahen Rocks

0   Mile   1

0   1
Kilometres

○ Tristan da Cunha

⬡ Inaccessible Island

⸰ Nightingale Island

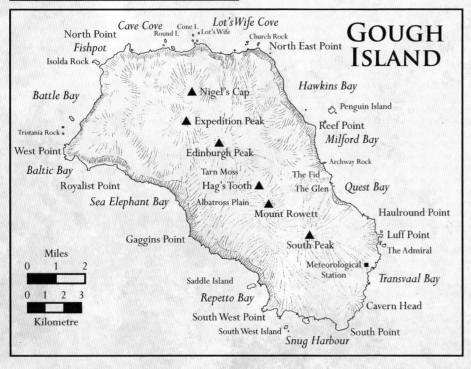

GOUGH ISLAND

Cave Cove   Cone I.   *Lot's Wife Cove*
North Point   Round I.   Lot's Wife
Fishpot   Church Rock
Isolda Rock   North East Point
Battle Bay   ▲ Nigel's Cap   *Hawkins Bay*
Tristania Rock   ▲ Expedition Peak   ⸰ Penguin Island
West Point   Reef Point
Baltic Bay   *Milford Bay*
▲ Edinburgh Peak   Archway Rock
Royalist Point   Tarn Moss   The Fid
Hag's Tooth ▲   The Glen   *Quest Bay*
Sea Elephant Bay   Albatross Plain ▲
▲ Mount Rowett   Haulround Point
Gaggins Point   Luff Point
▲ South Peak   The Admiral
Meteorological Station ■
Transvaal Bay
Saddle Island
Repetto Bay   Cavern Head
South West Point
South West Island   South Point
Snug Harbour

Miles
0   1   2

0   1   2   3
Kilometre

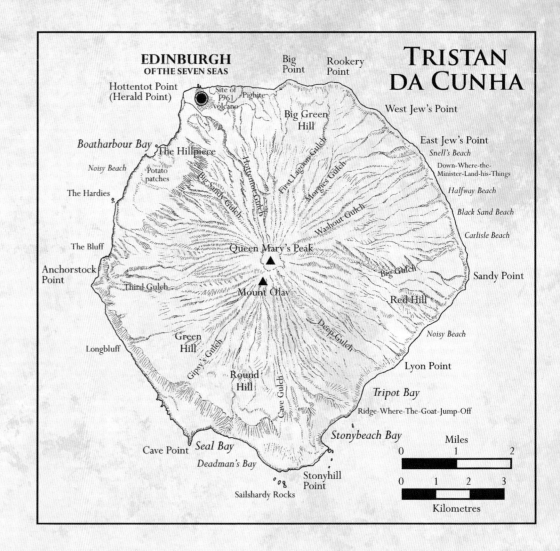

TRISTAN DA CUNHA

EDINBURGH
OF THE SEVEN SEAS
Big Point
Rookery Point
Hottentot Point (Herald Point)
Site of 1961 volcano
Pigbite
West Jew's Point
Big Green Hill
East Jew's Point
Boatharbour Bay
The Hillpiece
Snell's Beach
Noisy Beach
Potato patches
Down-Where-the-Minister-Land-his-Things
The Hardies
Halfway Beach
The Bluff
Black Sand Beach
Carlisle Beach
Queen Mary's Peak ▲
Anchorstock Point
Big Gulch
Sandy Point
Third Gulch
Mount Olav ▲
Red Hill
Green Hill
Noisy Beach
Longbluff
Lyon Point
Round Hill
Tripot Bay
Ridge-Where-The-Goat-Jump-Off
Stonybeach Bay
Cave Point
Seal Bay
Deadman's Bay
Stonyhill Point
Sailshardy Rocks

0   Miles   1   2

0   1   2   3
Kilometres

SOUTH ATLANTIC OCEAN

⬡ Gough Island

Edinburgh of the Seven Seas

This tiny village of about 250 inhabitants is a world unto its own. If it were London, its next nearest settlement would be Athens or Moscow! The Settlement is named after Prince Alfred, Duke of Edinburgh, in honour of his visit to the island in 1867. Among all the islanders there are currently nine surnames in use, the vast majority belonging to the Green (65 people), Swain (57), Repetto (42) and Glass (34) families, the fewest to recent arrivals Squibb (4) and Collins (1).

The economy of The Settlement is basic, depending on exports of native rock lobster, with just under 400 tonnes fished annually, and to a lesser degree on tourism, including provision of accommodation, guiding, the selling of souvenirs, and sales of stamps to collectors across the world. Prior to adopting the British pound as its currency, potatoes were the main currency on the island, and rare stamps can still be found that illustrate this: a 1946 stamp was issued bearing the local value of "4 potatoes"! Even so, until the 1960s few Tristanians ascribed value to possessions, and were more likely to freely share produce with each other, united in a sense of profound community spirit and a belief in the common good.

The Settlement was briefly evacuated in 1961 when the volcano erupted, sending lava perilously close to the village.

Edinburgh of the Seven Seas (Photo: Stewart McPherson).

A traditional Tristan dwelling (Photo: Stewart McPherson).

The eruption took place only a few hundred metres from Edinburgh of the Seven Seas. Photographed by the landing party from the frigate HMS Leopard (Imperial War Museum).

Dwarf tree ferns cover the slopes of the volcano (Photo: Stewart McPherson).

The majestic approach towards Tristan da Cunha (Photo: Stewart McPherson).

Landscape and Habitats

Tristan da Cunha is a 2062 metre high stratovolcano whose base lies 3700 metres below the surface of the sea. The archipelago formed as a result of upwelling magma from hotspots about 400 km east of the mid-Atlantic trench. The oldest and most weathered islands are in the Nightingale group (18 million years old), followed by Inaccessible island (6 million years) and Tristan itself (3 million years). Gough island, which lies 398 km southeast of the main island group, was formed from its own hotspot about 5 million years ago.

The islands all have a wet, cool-temperate oceanic climate with temperatures almost always in the 10–20 °C range. As a result, they are relatively lush, though being at 37° latitude, they are close to the Roaring Forties, with strong westerly winds and accompanying rain often battering the islands, keeping vegetation low and windswept, giving rise to a landscape that is very much reminiscent of Scotland, Ireland and Iceland.

Habitats are varied, ranging from rocky sea-cliffs to lowland meadows, with more sheltered areas giving rise to dwarf forests consisting of endemic trees and tree ferns which continue above the 500 metre elevation mark. Thereafter, the landscape starts to give way to more exposed landscapes, culminating in rocky lichen fields that periodically receive snow in winters.

Only moss and lichens grow on the barren upper slopes of Queen Mary's Peak (Rohan Holt).

The fertile plains outside of Edinburgh of the Seven Seas (Photo: Stewart McPherson).

An Atlantic yellow-nosed albatross (Photo: Stewart McPherson).

Atlantic yellow-nosed albatrosses feeding on fish scraps (Photo: Stewart McPherson).

Wildlife

The islands of the Tristan da Cunha archipelago are some of the most important in the world for their large breeding colonies of seabirds. In fact, two of the islands now comprise the UNESCO World Heritage Site of Gough and Inaccessible Islands, created to preserve their important birdlife. Initially encompassing only Gough island, the UNESCO site was later extended to include Inaccessible island and all of the maritime area lying within 12 miles of the two islands.

The spectacled petrel (*Procellaria conspicillata*) nests only on the western plateau of Inaccessible Island, while an additional seven species of bird are endemic to the islands, including the Gough finch and Gough island moorhen, the Inaccessible island rail and finch, the Nightingale island finch, the Grosbeak bunting and the Tristan thrush. The latter has evolved unusual vampiric tendencies in the harsh South Atlantic environment, stabbing the eggs albatrosses and shearwaters with their sharp beaks to extract their protein rich contents, killing nestlings and even drinking from the wounds and nibbling flesh from penguins injured by rough conditions in the sea!

Populations of other species, though not endemic, are very important, including the rare Atlantic yellow-nosed albatross, which follows local fishing boats to take advantage of by-catch tossed back into the sea.

The endemic Gough moorhen (*Gallinula comeri*) (Photo: Stewart McPherson).

The Tristan thrush (*Turdus eremita*) (Photo: Stuart Trowell).

A Tristan thrush feeding from a wounded penguin (Photo: Stewart McPherson).

Macaroni penguins muster close to the shore (Photo: Stewart McPherson).

On its own, Gough island is home to almost eight and a half million seabirds! These include at least 32 000 pairs of northern rockhopper penguins—though some estimates put the population at 65 000 pairs—as well as at least 2500 pairs of Tristan albatrosses, 5000 pairs of sooty albatrosses, 5000 pairs of aforementioned Atlantic yellow-nosed albatrosses, possibly as many as 1 750 000 pairs of two species of prions, 20 000 pairs of Kerguelen petrels, 20 000 pairs of the common diving petrel, 400 000 pairs of soft-plumaged petrels, 900 000 pairs of Atlantic petrels, 10 000 pairs of great-winged petrels, 10 000 pairs of grey petrels, 1 million pairs of great shearwaters, 20 000 pairs of little shearwaters, 10 000 pairs of grey-backed storm petrels, 10 000 pairs of white-faced storm petrels, 10 000 pairs of white-bellied storm petrels, 500 pairs of Antarctic terns (*Sterna vittata tristanensis*, a subspecies endemic to the Tristan Islands), 500 pairs of southern skuas, around 250 pairs of the southern giant petrel, 200 pairs of brown noddies and "several hundred pairs" of the blue petrel.

Extensive colonies of sub-Antarctic fur seals and elephant seals occur across the islands. These used to occur in such numbers that thousands were killed annually for their oil and pelts. The effects were catastrophic as animals were killed in unsustainable numbers. Since these species were afforded protection, their numbers have slowly risen close to historic levels.

Southern giant petrels (*Macronectes giganteus*) in a feeding frenzy (Photo: Shutterstock / Coolramblings).

The islanders of Tristan are acutely aware of the problems caused by introduced species, particularly cats, rats and mice, which decimated seabird populations on the mainland, driving the Tristan moorhen extinct in the late 1800s, and making it impossible for them to cultivate wheat. Today they are careful to maintain a quota on livestock to prevent soil erosion, and carry out annual ratting festivals where wild rats are caught and killed in order to protect seabirds and crops alike.

The introduction of mice to Gough island following a shipwreck in the 1800s had shocking consequences. Unlike on Tristan, where cats may prey upon the introduced rodents, mice arrived on Gough alone. In the absence of predators their population exploded and they stripped the island of seeds and wiped out endemic invertebrates. As food diminished, they turned their attentions to the seabirds, an abundant source of protein across the island.

Today, the mice of Gough island have developed a taste for flesh and have grown to giant proportions of 27 centimetres in length! At night they swarm over the birds' nests to consume their eggs and bite at the flanks of chicks and adults alike, exposing their flesh and internal organs. The severity of the problem is critical and proposals to eradicate the pests are being considered despite a cost of seven million pounds. Without appropriate action, Gough's nesting areas will fall silent as those on Ascension did centuries ago.

The Tristan albatross (*Diomedea dabbenena*) is endemic to the islands of the Tristan da Cunha group and the overwhelming majority (around 1500 pairs) breed on Gough Island (Photo: Ross Wanless and Andrea Angel).

The monster mice of Gough Island viciously bite and gnaw the sides of a Tristan albatross chick (Photo: Ross Wanless and Andrea Angel).

The remains of a Tristan albatross that has been killed and eaten by swarms of mice (Photo: Ross Wanless and Andrea Angel).

The endemic bog fern (Photo: Stewart McPherson).

Flora

The plants of the Tristan archipelago exhibit all the hallmarks of island endemism, with many taking on bizarre forms quite unlike those of their nearest relatives elsewhere. 53 species of flowering plant are recognised from across the islands, and 28 of those are endemic, along with a further 4 endemic subspecies. In addition to those are 38 species ferns and clubmosses, of which 15 species and 2 subspecies are regarded as endemic.

The only native tree in the archipelago is *Phylica arborea*, the island cape myrtle, found here and on Amsterdam Island in the southern Indian Ocean. Growing to 7–8 metres in height, in most places it is dwarfed by the exposed conditions. Also widespread in the islands is the endemic bog fern, *Blechnum palmiforme*, which forms thick, palm-tree like stems up to 1.6 metres tall, topped with a crown of long fronds with thick, leathery leaves capable of withstanding the windy weather.

In more exposed areas, particularly high elevation sites such as the flanks of the volcano (Queen Mary's Peak), a number of endemic tufted grasses occur, including the small bog grasses *Scirpus bicolor* and *Deschampsia mejlandii*. Eventually, these give way to the toughest photosynthetic organisms of all, the various species of moss and lichen that cling to the rocks at the summit of the volcano weathering snow and intense sunlight year round.

The bog fern forms small, palm like growths (Photo: Stewart McPherson).

Ground vegetation, including the berries of diddle-dee (Photo: Stewart McPherson).

Marine Environment

The marine environment of Tristan underpins much of its life on land. In particular, the birds that crowd the cliffs and plateaus of the various islands, as well as the seals that line their beaches, all depend on the ocean for food. Nutrient rich upwellings of cold water from the deep ocean feeds plankton around the islands, in turn feeding small fish and their larger predators as well as baleen whales.

The island's population of native rock lobster (*Jasus paulensis*) is one of the densest in the world, allowing for a relatively large catch from a comparatively small but certainly pristine and unpolluted area, seeing it sold overseas as a highly exclusive export.

Amongst the most beautiful sights in Tristan's waters is its forests of giant kelp that clothe the island's rocky shallows. Continually moving shafts of light shine through the long strands of swaying, yellowish brown kelp, each frond dragged upwards by the inflated buoys at their bases. Giant kelp (*Macrocystis pyrifera*) is a spectacular brown seaweed that grows to 60 m or more in length. The species boasts one of the highest growth rates of any organism on the planet and the fronds of this spectacular algae have been recorded to grow at more than half a metre per day! Witnessing seals and Rockhopper penguins swimming through this kelp forest is truly mesmerising.

Giant kelp forests below the waves (Photo: Rohan Holt).

Seals at play amongst beds of kelp (Photo: Rohan Holt).

King penguins on the Falkland Islands (Photo: Kwest/Shutterstock.com).

Population: 3398 (2016)
Area: 12 173 sq. km of dry land
Currency: Falkland Islands pound
Capital: Stanley
Flag: A Blue Ensign bearing the seal of the islands—a ram (representing the livestock that once roamed the islands) over John Davis's ship *Desire*.

FALKLAND ISLANDS

The Falkland Islands are located in the South Atlantic approximately 400 kilometres northeast of the tip of Tierra del Fuego and about 1220 kilometres north of the Antarctic Peninsula. The Islands consist of two main islands, East and West Falkland, separated by the Falkland Sound, and approximately 776 smaller islands and islets nearby. East Falkland is the site of the Islands' capital, Stanley, where the vast majority of the population live, while the rest of the Islands are referred to as the 'Camp', a sparsely populated region of farms and isolated settlements.

The Islands are named after the Falkland Sound, which received its name in 1690 by naval captain John Strong who made the first recorded landing on the Islands in that year. The title was given to commemorate Anthony Cary, 5th Viscount of Falkland (a village and former royal burgh in Scotland) who part-owned Strong's ship, the HMS *Welfare*. However, the name was only extended to the whole group of islands in 1708, when the privateer Woodes Rogers used—for the very first time—the standard modern name "Falkland Islands" in his logbook on 24 December. The Spanish name for the islands, "Las Malvinas", is derived from the French name "Isles Malouines", which was coined by the French Geographer Royal Guillaume Delisle in 1720 when merchants from the French port of Saint Malo passed the Islands on their way to trade in Chile. The French name passed into Spanish as "Islas Maluinas", which became "Islas Malvinas" in the early 19th century. The name Malvinas is still used by Argentinians, though Spanish speakers of other nationalities often use the term Islas Falklands.

Although Captain Strong is often attributed the first recorded landing on the Islands, the Islands were first documented on a pair of maps drawn in 1518–1519. Their Portuguese originators are believed to have been the first to have sighted and set foot upon them. In the 1520s, they were marked on a number of Spanish maps, while a Spanish ship was blown into the Islands in the 1540s, its logbook indicating that some months were spent there to effect repairs. They were also visited by the English in 1592, when the *Desire*, a ship captained by explorer John Davis, was blown by a storm into the Islands, and again in 1594 by explorer Sir Richard Hawkins named them "Hawkins Maiden-land" after himself and Queen Elizabeth I.

The Islands were first settled in the 1760s, when the French landed settlers on East Falkland in 1764, while the British Royal Navy landed on Saunders Island off West Falkland in 1765, taking possession of the archipelago for the British Crown and naming the harbour there Port Egmont. The British and French settlers remained on good terms, but in 1767 France surrendered its settlement to Spain and the Spanish captured Port Egmont. This sparked the brief First Falklands Crisis (1770–1771), but saw Port Egmont returned to the British to avoid war. Formal British rule of the island was formally reasserted in 1833 after a period of absence starting in 1774.

Falkland Islands

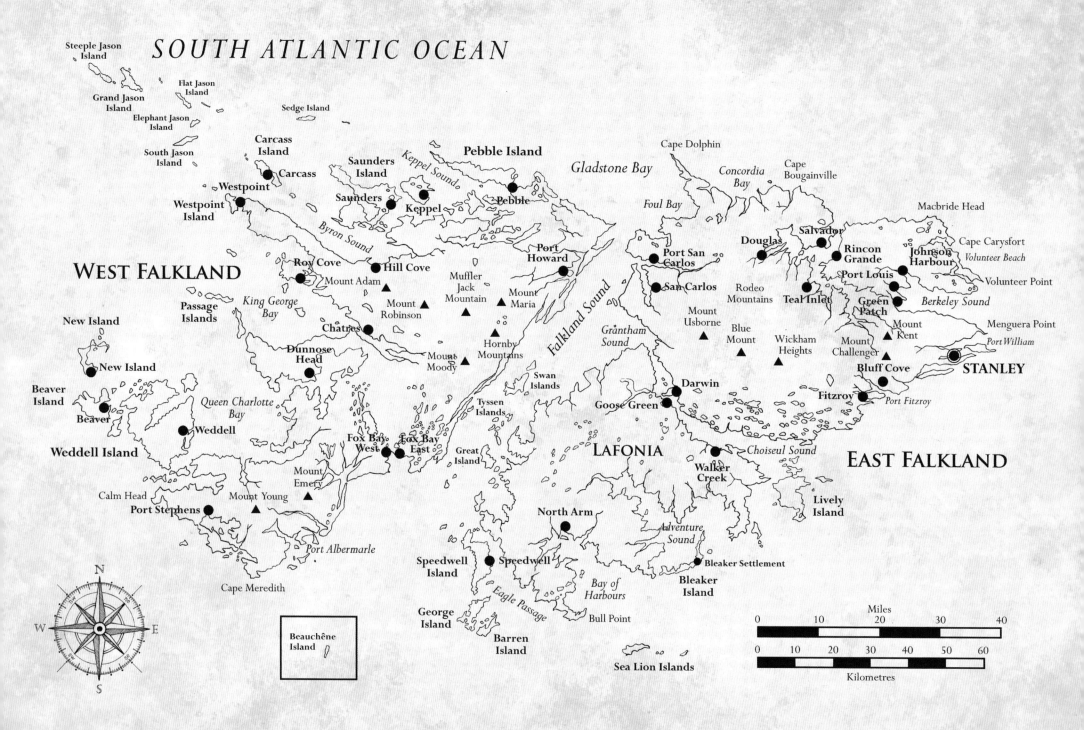

Stanley

Stanley is the capital of the Falkland Islands and home to 85% of the Islands' population. The town, named after Lord Edward Smith-Stanley, is the commercial and government centre of the Islands and also the hub for tourism, boasting hotels and motels, along with many pubs and restaurants.

The town was established as the capital in 1845 on account of its deep water anchorage, soon becoming a major repair stop for ships traversing the Magellan Straits, as well as a major base for whaling and seal hunting in the Southern Ocean, remains of which can still be seen. Today, Stanley is a surprisingly diverse, cosmopolitan and modern community of predominantly professional, government, fishing and tourism industry related workers with one of the top-10 highest per capita GDPs in the world.

Argentina invaded Stanley on April 2nd, 1982, aiming to seize the Islands from the U.K., initiating the Falklands War. The town was occupied for 10 weeks until the surrender of Argentina on June 14th. The effects of the war can still be seen, with some land off-limits because of uncleared Argentine land mines, and ruins of downed helicopters still visible. The U.K. aims to clear all mines by the end of 2019. The war has driven investment in the Islands and led to the embedding of self-determination in the Islands' constitution. The islanders voted to remain British in a 2013 referendum.

Houses in Stanley, capital of the Falklands (Photo: Stewart McPherson).

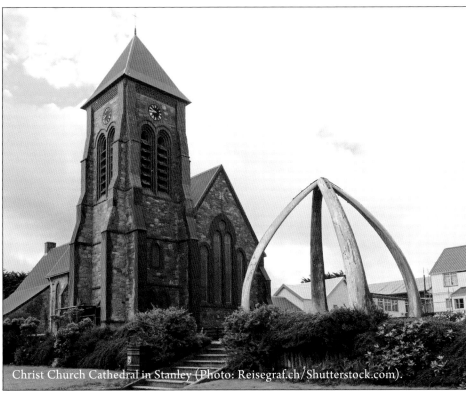

Christ Church Cathedral in Stanley (Photo: Reisegraf.ch/Shutterstock.com).

Relicts of the Falklands War litter the islands (Photo: Stewart McPherson).

Landscape and Habitats

The Falkland Islands are the fragmented remains of continental crust that remain from the break-up of Gondwana, an ancient supercontinent that started to break up 184 million years ago, giving rise to the South Atlantic ocean. The landscape is predominantly hilly, the rugged prominences appearing mountainous but actually being relatively low—the highest point in the Islands is Mount Usborne at just 705 metres in height.

The climate of the Falklands has been warming during recorded history, and is currently classified as sub-polar oceanic climate, with cool summers (average 14 ºC) and mild winters (average 5 ºC), the fairly narrow temperature range the result of buffering by the surrounding ocean. Rainfall is moderate, about 544 mm per year, and falls year round with a slight decrease from August to November during the southern winter.

The landscape of the two large islands is dominated by plains of grassy heath and bogs, with much of the large, native tussac grass having disappeared. Important patches remain on offshore islands where both man and introduced species have had less of an impact. The heavily indented coastline and hundreds of small islands mean that the Falklands have an estimated 1300 kilometres of coast, which ranges from rocky headlands to spectacular white beaches, some of which are home to vast bird colonies.

A rocky peak in the Falklands (Photo: Kwest/Shutterstock.com).

Tussac grass vegetation on Kidney island (Photo: Stewart McPherson).

Beautiful white beaches in Gypsy Cove (Photo: Cheryl Ramalho/Shutterstock.com).

Macaroni penguins line a rocky shoreline (Photo: Simon Vacher).

A large colony of imperial shags (Photo: Jeremy Richards/Shutterstock.com).

Black-browed albatrosses (Photo: Riesegraf.ch/Shutterstock.com).

Feeding young (Photo: Stewart McPherson).

An imperial shag (Photo: J. Richards/Shutterstock.com).

Striated caracaras, the native raptor (Photo: Jeremy Richards/Shutterstock.com).

A striated caracara feeding (Photo: Ondrej Prosicky/Shutterstock.com).

Wildlife

There are no native reptiles or amphibians in the Falklands, and the only native land mammal, the 'warrah', is now extinct. A total of 227 bird species are recorded from the islands, of which two are endemic, and some of the most impressive bird colonies on the planet can be found here—including 500 000 pairs of black-browed albatross—alongside large populations of marine mammals, particularly seals.

Of extreme importance are the seasonal nesting stations of five species of penguins, namely the gentoo, king, macaroni, Magellanic and southern rockhopper penguins—a total of around one million birds visit each year! The breeding colonies of gentoo penguins are the largest in the world for that species, with about 130 000 estimated to visit annually. Charles Darwin himself studied the birds of the island, writing admirably of their tough nature. Seals and penguins were once hunted close to extinction across the islands for their oil, with 30 000 seals taken annually in the late 1800s, and about 500 000 penguins in 1867 alone. Fortunately, all are now strictly protected with significant recoveries noted.

A native raptor, the striated caracara (*Phalcoboenus australis*) is notable for being a comedic and fearless kleptomaniac, stealing any colourful objects it can find to study, favouring red since it apparently resembles meat!

A gentoo penguin colony, Bleeker Island (Photo: Jeremy Richards/Shutterstock.com).

The endemic flightless steamer duck (Photo: David Osborn/Shutterstock.com).

The two endemic bird species are the Cobb's wren (*Troglodytes cobbi*) and the Falkland flightless steamer duck (*Tachyeres brachypterus*), which occur alongside at least 13 endemic subspecies.

Two centuries ago, the Islands were home to an abundant endemic canid called the warrah, or Falkland Islands wolf (*Dusicyon australis*). Darwin observed this fox-like animal, writing in 1839 "These wolves are well known [for] their tameness and curiosity; which the sailors, who ran into the water to avoid them, mistook for fierceness." In the same piece, he predicted that the animal would soon "be classed with the dodo, as an animal which has perished from the face of the Earth." Seen as a danger to lambs, the animals were actively hunted such that the species was already absent from tracts of land by the time Darwin arrived.

Darwin's prediction came true in 1876, when the last known warrah was shot dead at Shallow Bay, West Falkland, resulting in the first known extinction of any canid in recorded history.

The only native mammals remaining in the Falklands are marine, including massive elephant seals, which may way up to 5 tonnes and exceed 6 metres in length, as well as smaller leopard seals, Ross seals and fur seals. The South American sea lion (*Otaria flavescens*), which are widely distributed across South America, also breeds on the Islands.

The extinct warrah, or "Falklands wolf" (illustration by John Gerrard Keulemans, from George Mivart's *Dogs, Jackals, Wolves, and Foxes: A Monograph of the Candidae*, published by R. H. Porter, London, 1890).

A rare skull of the extinct warrah (Photo: Simon Vacher).

A southern sea lion bull and female (Photo: David Osborn/Shutterstock.com).

A male southern elephant seal (Photo: Fieldwork/Shutterstock.com).

Female elephant seals at rest (Photo: Ondrej Prosicky/Shutterstock.com).

Flowers and berries of diddle-dee (Photo: Stewart McPherson).

Flora

The Falkland Islands have no native trees, and most of the vegetation is composed of grasses, shrubs and ferns. Prominent plants include the conspicuous *Empetrum rubrum*, a red berried shrub that also grows on Tristan da Cunha, in Chile and in Argentina. In the Falklands, this species is known as diddle-dee, its edible berries traditionally used to make a tart jam by the Islanders. About another 360 vascular plants are found on the Islands, 170 of which are native and 14 endemic.

Endemic plants include a species of beautiful lady slipper (*Calceolaria fothergillii*), the bizarre-looking snake plant (*Nassauvia serpens*) and the endangered pin-cushion like false plantain (*Nastanthus falklandicus*) a shore plant with an extremely restricted range. One of the native species is a carnivorous sundew, *Drosera uniflora*, which traps, kills and digests insects with its sticky leaves.

Originally covering the littoral areas of much of the Islands, tussac grass (*Poa flabellata*) is now mostly restricted to off-shore Islands where it may form colonies so dense that few other plants can compete with it. The grass grows 2–4 metres in height, forming large tussocks that can survive for centuries. Old growth tussac is a vital habitat for a large number of birds, native invertebrates and even sea lions, its decline disastrous for many species.

The Vanilla daisy (*Leuceria suaveolens*) growing in the Falkland Islands (Photo: Shutterstock.com / Umomos).

Drosera uniflora, a native carnivorous plant (Photo: Stewart McPherson).

Marine Environment

The waters around the Falkland Islands are rich as a result of cold currents which rise from the depths bringing with them abundant nutrients. As a result, a broad diversity of animals can be found in association with the Islands' waters, especially sea birds and sea mammals, like seals and sea lions, but also cetaceans, including southern right whales, humpbacks, giant blue whales, fin whales, sei whales and sperm whales. Many of these species were targeted historically by whalers, with a shore-based whaling station established on New Island, West Falkland, in 1909. Operations in these waters were never on the scale of those of the highly successful whaling operations on South Georgia and the whaling station was closed in 1917.

Alongside the great whales of the Falklands are found the rare Commerson's dolphin, one of the smallest dolphins in the world, as well as killer whales and Peale's dolphins.

The cold water also provides a refuge to giant species of kelp. The kelp found in the waters of the Falklands may reach 30 metres in length, forming vast, dense forests that may spread over several square kilometres. Given the marked population decline in kelp in northern waters in recent years owing to warming of the world's oceans, the apparent good health of these kelp beds may become increasingly important.

The waters of the Falkland Islands are home to forests of giant bladder kelp (*Macrocystis pyrifera*) (Photo: Shallow Marine Surveys Group).

The rocky reefs of the Falkland Islands harbour high biodiversity (Photo: Shallow Marine Surveys Group).

Commerson's dolphins playing in the surf (Photo: Fieldwork/Shutterstock.com).

A king penguin colony on South Georgia (Photo: Rich Lindie/ Shutterstock.com).

Population: No permanent population
Area: 3903 sq. km, 90% snow covered
Currency: British pound
Capital: King Edward Point
Flag: A Blue Ensign bearing the islands' coat of arms—a shield with the lion of England and stars of Captain Cook, supported by a fur seal, a macaroni penguin and a reindeer.

SOUTH GEORGIA AND THE SOUTH SANDWICH ISLANDS

The remote Overseas Territory of South Georgia and the South Sandwich Islands (SGSSI) comprise two geographically and geologically distinct island groups located in the South Atlantic about 1350 and 2080 m east and east southeast of the Falkland Islands respectively. South Georgia, a mountainous remnant of uplifted continental fragment rising to 2934 m at its highest point, is the largest island in the two groups. It is about 165 km long and mostly 20–30 km wide, with nine small offshore islands and three significant isolated rock outcrops, the most distant of which is almost 200 km to the southeast. The eleven principal South Sandwich Islands are all volcanic and sit in an arc situated about 620 km to the southeast of South Georgia, and include a number of minor offshore outcrops. The largest of the South Sandwich islands is Montagu, with an area of 110 sq. km and a peak 1370 m high. None of these inhospitable islands have permanent populations, but scientific and government staff occupy a number of facilities on South Georgia, including research facilities at King Edward Point and a British Antarctic Survey station on Bird Island.

The first reliable sighting of South Georgia was made by English merchant Anthony de la Roché in 1675, when his ship ventured off course in storms after rounding Cape Horn. Roché anchored in one of South Georgia's southern bays for a fortnight before sailing to and landing on Gough Island (Tristan da Cunha). The first recorded landing on South Georgia was made by Captain James Cook on 17 January 1775. He claimed sovereignty over the territory in the name of the Kingdom of Great Britain, naming the new land "the Isle of Georgia" in honour of King George III. In his log, Cook described the desolate island as *"savage and horrible... the wild rocks raised their lofty summits until they were lost in the clouds, and the valleys lay buried in everlasting snow."* After mapping the island, Cook sailed to the southeast where he discovered the southern eight of the Sandwich Islands, naming them "Sandwich Land" in honour of John Montagu, 4th Earl of Sandwich and First Lord of the Admiralty. Cook was evidently keen to impress Lord Sandwich, for he also bestowed the name "Sandwich Islands" to the Hawaiian Islands, the uninhabited Manuae atoll in the Cook Islands of the South Pacific and also Efate Island in the Republic of Vanuatu! The word "South" was later added to distinguish the South Atlantic group from the others.

The Government of South Georgia by Britain was instituted in 1843, with South Sandwich added in 1908. Both were thereafter governed as Falklands dependencies until 1985 when, prompted by the brief seizure of the islands by Argentina in 1982 and the Falklands War that followed, the Territory of "South Georgia and the South Sandwich Islands" was created. Today, the islands are administered from Stanley, in the Falkland Islands.

South Georgia

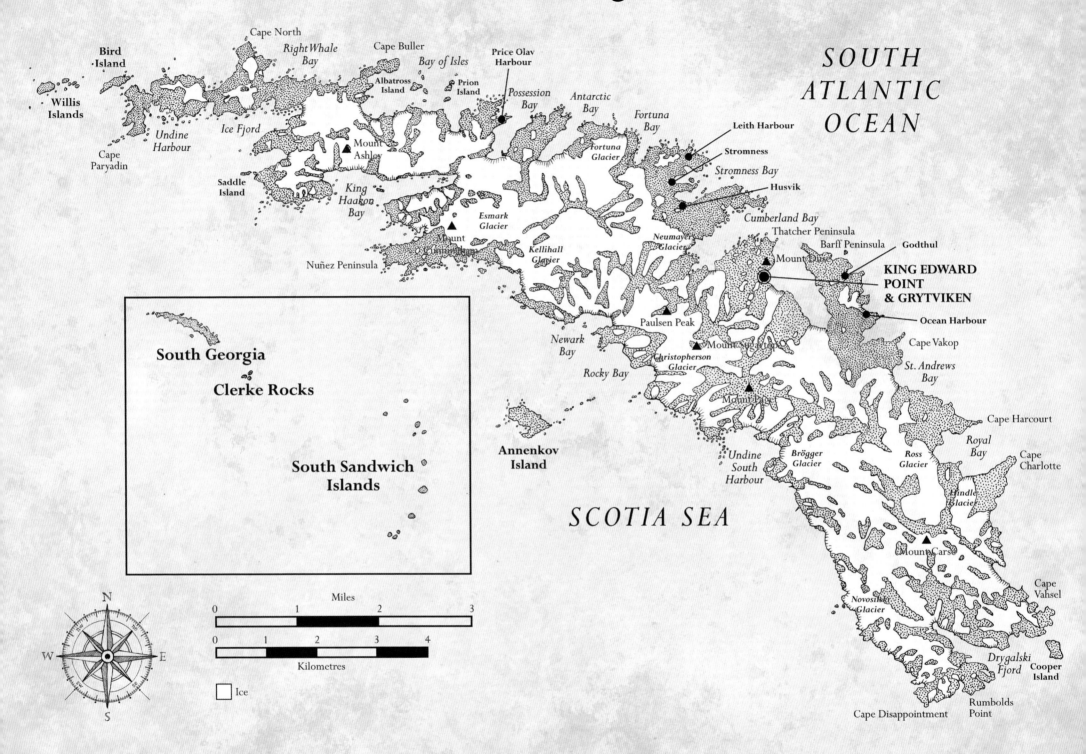

SOUTH ATLANTIC OCEAN

SCOTIA SEA

Bird Island

Willis Islands

Cape Paryadin

Undine Harbour

Saddle Island

Cape North

Right Whale Bay

Ice Fjord

King Haakon Bay

Nuñez Peninsula

Mount Ashley

Esmark Glacier

Mount Cunningham

Cape Buller

Albatross Island

Bay of Isles

Prion Island

Price Olav Harbour

Possession Bay

Antarctic Bay

Fortuna Bay

Fortuna Glacier

Kellihall Glacier

Neumayer Glacier

Leith Harbour

Stromness

Stromness Bay

Husvik

Cumberland Bay

Thatcher Peninsula

Barff Peninsula

Godthul

Mount Duse

KING EDWARD POINT & GRYTVIKEN

Ocean Harbour

Cape Vakop

St. Andrews Bay

Paulsen Peak

Newark Bay

Rocky Bay

Christopherson Glacier

Mount Sugartop

Mount Paget

Undine South Harbour

Brögger Glacier

Ross Glacier

Royal Bay

Cape Harcourt

Cape Charlotte

Hindle Glacier

Mount Carse

Cape Vahsel

Novosilski Glacier

Drygalski Fjord

Cooper Island

Cape Disappointment

Rumbolds Point

Annenkov Island

South Georgia

Clerke Rocks

South Sandwich Islands

N W E S

Miles
0 1 2 3

Kilometres
0 1 2 3 4

Ice

Giant petrels eating a king penguin chick (Photo: Robert McGillivray/Shutterstock.com).

King penguins in Fortuna Bay, South Georgia (Photo: Artincamera/Shutterstock.com).

A vast king penguin colony close to the shore, South Georgia (Photo: Rich Lindie/Shutterstock.com).

A historic image of Grytviken whaling station on South Georgia (Nigel Bonner).

King Edward Point

Named around 1906 after King Edward VII, this tiny settlement serves as capital of the territory and is comprised of several modern research and accommodation buildings, as well as the historic buildings; Discovery House (1925) and the former Gaol (1912). The population comprises British Antarctic Survey staff, two government officers and their partners, and several summer staff from the museum and Post Office at nearby Grytviken.

Grytviken is the most visited site in the Territory, being the site of former whaling operations across SGSSI, a once highly lucrative industry. Whaling was, in fact, preceded by seal hunting in the islands. When Captain Cook visited and mapped the islands in 1775, they were home to an estimated 2–3 million Antarctic fur seals (*Arctocephalus gazella*) as well as many elephant seals (*Mirounga leonina*). These were hunted indiscriminately, with 1 200 000 seals killed for their pelts by 1825. By 1920, the fur seal was declared commercially extinct, with only a few hundred remaining.

Whalers followed the sealers in 1904, building a whale processing station at Grytviken that was soon followed by six others around the island. During the 61 years of its operation, Grytviken alone processed 53 761 dead whales. It was the last whaling station to close, ceasing to operate in 1966 only because so few whales were left to hunt in the Southern Ocean.

The carcass of a sperm whale being 'flensed' for its blubber.

Remains of a vessel at Grytviken whaling station (Photo: Stewart McPherson).

Landscape and Habitats

The islands of South Georgia and South Sandwich are predominantly mountainous and rocky, consisting of precipitous, permanently ice-clad peaks, the lower, more maritime coastal areas becoming free of snow during the warmer summer months. South Georgia has 11 peaks over 2000 metres, most in the backbone chain of mountain ranges running the length of the island. Most mountains are separated by huge glaciers and ice caps.

The climate of the islands is classified as polar though, being surrounded by ocean, extremes of temperature are not the norm, with summers usually between 2 and 9 ^{o}C and winters between -5 and +1 ^{o}C. However, the weather can be harsh, with frequent cloud cover, precipitation and strong, westerly winds, making for a formidable environment. To this end, no trees or shrubs are present on the island.

The few habitats available to plants and animals occur at lower elevations, particularly on stony and gravelly terrain created by receding glaciers close to the sea. Beaches, cliffs and coastal lowlands are important habitats for some of the largest bird and seal populations on the planet, being home to albatrosses, various species of petrels and penguins, numerous other seabirds, fur seals and elephant seals.

Mountainous landscape of South Georgia (Photo: Anton Ivanov/Shutterstock.com).

A glacier enters the sea at Drygalski Fjord (Photo: Cheryl Ramalho/Shutterstock.com).

Windswept vegetation is mainly restricted to the coast (Photo: Stewart McPherson).

King penguins and their chicks on the Salisbury Plain of South Georgia (Photo: Tetyana Dotsenko/Shutterstock.com).

Moulting chicks (Photo: T. Dotsenko/Shutterstock.com).

Adult and young (Photo: Rich Lindie/Shutterstock.com).

Adult penguin (Photo: R. McGillivray/Shutterstock.com).

Wildlife

South Georgia and most of the more northern South Sandwich Islands remain free of sea ice during winter. As a result, these pin-pricks of land in the vastness of the South Atlantic attract many species from across the Southern Ocean to breed. Massive numbers of animals occupy the beaches and hinterland of the islands, representing some of the greatest concentrations of large animals on Earth.

The largest of all colonies on South Georgia are those of penguins, which total 7 million. The St Andrew's Bay king penguin colony is the largest of this species with almost 300 000 birds, while another colony at Salisbury Plain is home to at least 200 000 birds. About 1.1 million pairs of macaroni penguins and thousands of long-tailed gentoo and chinstrap penguins also cover the island's hillsides, such as at Hercules Bay. The largest penguin colony in the world, with 2 million chinstrap penguins, occurs at Zavodovski Island, a large volcano in the South Sandwich Islands.

Coastal habitats are frequented by other bird species, including brown skuas and giant petrels, both of which feed on young or injured penguins. The endemic South Georgia Pintail is an omnivorous duck that scavenges on seal carcasses, while even the endemic South Georgia pipit, a small (sparrow-sized) songbird, may also snatch carrion to survive!

Gentoo penguins (Photo: Anton Ivanov/Shutterstock.com).

Macaroni penguins (Photo: Charles Bergman/Shutterstock.com).

The macaroni has amazing head feathers (Photo: James Stone/Shutterstock.com).

Wandering albatrosses (Photo: MZPhoto.CZ/Shutterstock.com).

In total, 31 bird species nest on South Georgia and the South Sandwich Island. Many are far less conspicuous than the penguins and large elegant albatrosses, and are often overlooked, despite their great numbers. These smaller birds include 22 million pairs of Antarctic prions, 3.8 million pairs of common diving petrels, 2 million pairs of endemic South Georgian diving petrels, 600 000 thousand pairs of Wilson's storm petrels and 2 million pairs of the larger white-chinned petrel.

Despite being hunted almost to extinction by 1920, fur seals now occur in great numbers once more on the beaches of both archipelagos. From 1908 to the mid-1960s, the British government introduced legislation to protect all breeding grounds of the Antarctic fur seal in the South Atlantic Ocean, eventually banning seal hunting entirely. This allowed the fur seal population to recover, and enabled the species to increase rapidly around South Georgia and repopulate the South Sandwich Islands. Elephant seals are also numerous once more, and the massive bulls of this species engage in violent, bloody and sometimes fatal competitive bouts during the breeding season, in which the victors win the right to mate with local harems of females.

Reindeer were introduced to South Georgia as game by whalers during the early 20th century, but they caused major damage to the vegetation of the island and were successfully eradicated in 2015.

Fur seals on the Salisbury Plain (Photo: Goldilock Project/Shutterstock.com).

A grooming fur seal pup (Photo: nwdph/Shutterstock.com).

A female elephant seal (Photo: Jo Crebbin/Shutterstock.com).

An elephant seal pup (Photo: Hullis/Shutterstock.com).

Hydromedion sparsatum, one of several species of native tussac beetle (Photo: Roger Key).

Yellow-billed pintain duck (Photo: Jo Crebbin/Shutterstock.com).

Fur seals amongst tussac grass (Photo: Danita Delmont/Shutterstock.com).

Flora

With no trees or shrubs amongst the native flora, the islands of this Overseas Territory appear almost devoid of vegetation. In floristic terms they are classed as tundra, areas where tree growth is prevented by severe conditions, especially the short growing seasons and low summer temperatures.

Only two species of flowering plant occur in the South Sandwich Islands, the vegetation being almost exclusively of mosses, liverworts and lichens. However, on South Georgia there are 27 native vascular plants. These include six grass species, four species of rush, six types of fern, one species each of sedge and clubmoss, and nine species of small, herbaceous flowering plants. Tussac (*Poa flabellata*), a species of coastal tussock-forming grass can attain heights of 2.5 metres, is the largest plant. There are also wet grasslands, dry grasslands, bogs overlying deep peat, herbfields, and, at higher elevations on loose stone, fellfield, sparsely colonised mainly by mosses and lichens. At least 76 non-native plant species have been recorded, of which about 41 currently persist; most were introduced unintentionally in building materials and in fodder for livestock at the whaling stations.

Far greater numbers of non-vascular plants are recorded, amongst which are almost 130 moss species and 85 species of liverwort. Also, about 200 species of lichen have been documented, as well as with many fungi.

Greater burnet plants (*Acaena magellanica*) produce seed heads containing seeds which have a barbed spine to attach to animals for dispersal (Photo: Deirdre Galbraith).

The inconspicuous flowers of the Antarctic buttercup (*Ranunculus biternatus*) (Photo: Ronald Lewis-Smith).

Marine Environment

Recent research has attempted to map the marine biogeography of the islands, revealing that the South Georgian shelf is the most species rich region of the Southern Ocean recorded to date. A remarkable 17 732 different species have been recorded, with 35% of those noted only once, and 85% noted fewer than ten times, an indication of how rare many of the species are. With animals ranging from microscopic plankton and dainty sea butterflies (shell-less, free swimming sea snails) to the largest animal on earth (the blue whale), the value of these waters is immeasurable. The waters of the Territory are designated as a Marine Protected Area.

Historic whaling was an ecological disaster, with most species hunted to the point of extermination. As the largest species, the blue was the most profitable and amongst the most intensively hunted. Marine biologists estimate that the original blue whale population was about 300 000 individuals. When the last whaling station closed on South Georgia in 1966, only about 1000 blue whales remained in all of the seas and oceans of the world.

It is estimated that if the whaling stations and factory ships had operated for just one more year, the global blue whale population would have been reduced beyond recovery. The largest animal ever to have lived on Earth would now be extinct.

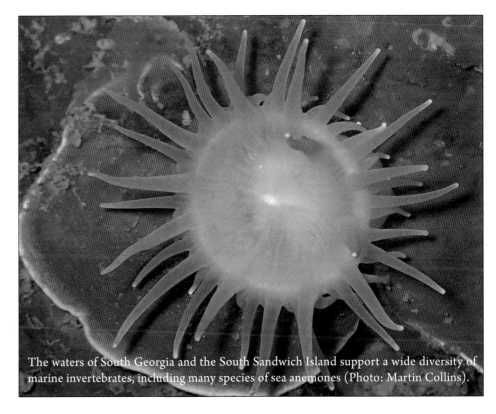

The waters of South Georgia and the South Sandwich Island support a wide diversity of marine invertebrates, including many species of sea anemones (Photo: Martin Collins).

An image showing one of the largest of all blue whales killed at South Georgia, to supply the whaling industry. (Photo: Frank Hurley / National Library of Australia).

A towering iceberg dwarfs a small research vessel (Photo: Will Ng).

Population: none permanent
Area: 1 709 400 sq. km of dry land
Currency: British pound
Capital: N/A
Flag: A white ensign with the Territory's coat of arms—a shield with a torch of discovery supported by the lion of England and an Emperor penguin.

BRITISH ANTARCTIC TERRITORY

Consisting of over 1 700 000 square kilometres of land, the British Antarctic Territory is the largest of the UK Overseas Territories. The territory comprises the entire region south of latitude 60° S between longitudes 20° W and 80° W, forming a wedge that extends to the South Pole itself. The Antarctic Peninsula occurs within the area of the territory, which includes all nearby islands including the South Shetland Islands (including Elephant and Deception islands) and the South Orkney Islands.

Over 99% of the British Antarctic Territory's land surface consists of permanent ice. This is mainly in the form of glaciers or ice sheets up to five kilometres deep. Virtually all of the icy landscape is featureless and sterile. The small area of land that is free of ice during the summer mainly consists of coastal outcrops—particularly along the peninsula and its islands—and, to a far lesser extent, the tips of mountains that poke through the ice sheet. The coastal areas are magnets for wildlife, though Antarctica's diversity of plants and animals is the lowest of all continents on Earth. During winter, the surface waters surrounding Antarctica freeze in all directions for up to 1,600 km. The formation of sea ice effectively doubles the size of the continent, all but disappearing in summer!

The continent of Antarctica was first sighted on 28 January 1820 by Fabian von Bellingshausen and Mikhail Lazarev, each the commander of a pair of ships charged by the Imperial Russian Navy with finding land at the South Pole. The first confirmed landing was conducted by a team of Norwegians in 1895, however the United Kingdom was the first country to lay claim to any part of Antarctica. Having had a continuous presence in the Antarctic region since 1833, when it reasserted sovereignty over the Falkland Islands, the UK extended its claims to include the British Antarctic Territory in 1908.

The claim is based on the UK's long-standing influence within the regions south of the Falkland Islands and South Georgia. Many of the earliest explorers of the continent were British, becoming leading figures in the 'Heroic Age of Antarctic Exploration'. Most notable among them were Robert Falcon Scott—who led the first successful foray to the Antarctic Plateau in December of 1902, and the ultimately fatal first British expedition to the South Pole, which arrived on 17 January 1912, just over four weeks after Norway's Roald Amundsen became the first person to reach the pole—as well as Ernest Shackleton, Edward Wilson, Frank Wild, William Lashly and Irish explorer Tom Crean. The Antarctic Peninsula has been continuously manned by the UK since 1943, following the establishment of permanently occupied British bases in the territory.

A 1959 Antarctic Treaty, enforced from 1961, effectively suspended all territorial claims and set the continent of Antarctica aside for science, conservation and peaceful use.

British Antarctic Territory

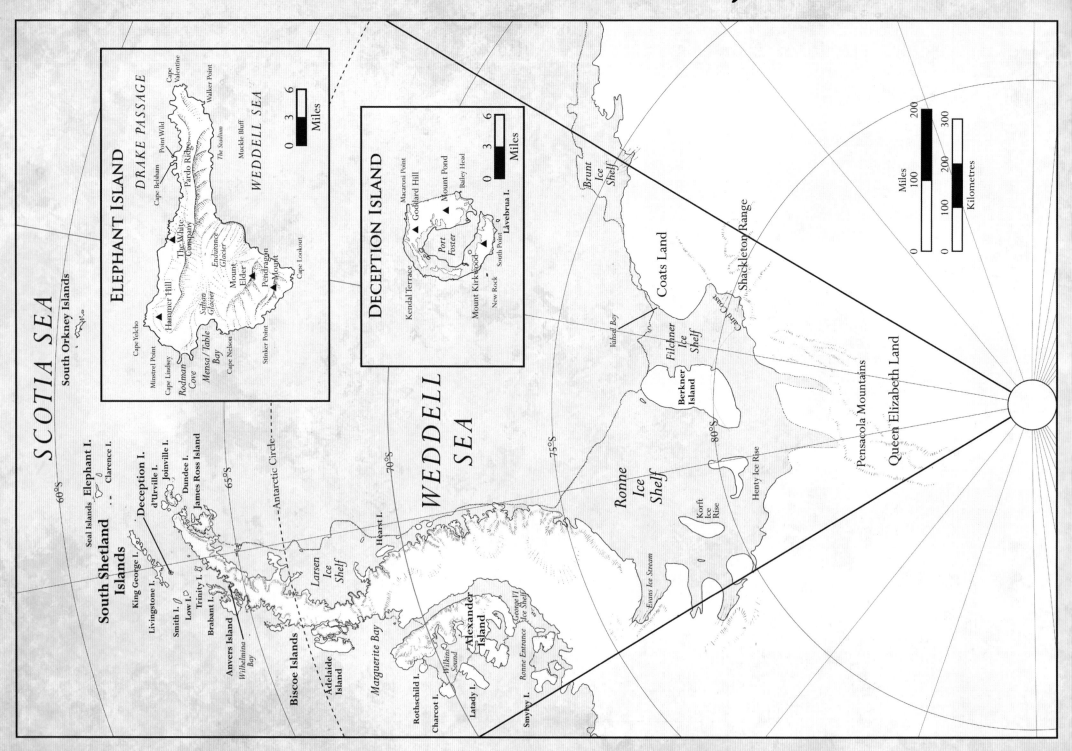

ELEPHANT ISLAND

DRAKE PASSAGE

Cape Valentine
Walker Point
Cape Wild
Point Wild
Pardo Ridge
The Stadium
Cape Belsham
Muckle Bluff

WEDDELL SEA

The White Company
Hammer Hill
Endurance Glacier
Mount Elder
Pendragon Mount
Cape Lookout

Cape Yelcho
Minstrel Point
Cape Lindsey
Rodman Cove
Sultan Glacier
Mensa / Table Bay
Cape Nelson
Stinker Point

0 3 6
Miles

DECEPTION ISLAND

Macaroni Point
Goddard Hill
Mount Pond
Bailey Head
Kendal Terrace
Port Foster
Mount Kirkwood
Lávebrua I.
New Rock
South Point

0 3 6
Miles

Brunt Ice Shelf

Coats Land

Shackleton Range

Vahsel Bay

Filchner Ice Shelf

Berkner Island

Pensacola Mountains

Queen Elizabeth Land

80°S

SCOTIA SEA

South Orkney Islands

Seal Islands
Elephant I.
Clarence I.

South Shetland Islands

King George I.
Livingstone I.
Smith I.
Low I.
Trinity I.
Brabant I.
Deception I.
d'Urville I.
Joinville I.
Dundee I.
James Ross Island

Antarctic Circle

65°S

70°S

75°S

WEDDELL SEA

Romne Ice Shelf

Korff Ice Rise

Henty Ice Rise

Evans Ice Stream

60°S

Anvers Island
Wilhelmina Bay

Biscoe Islands

Adelaide Island

Marguerite Bay

Rothschild I.
Charcot I.
Latady I.
Smyley I.

Alexander Island

Wilkins Sound

George VI Ice Shelf

Ronne Entrance

Hearst I.

Larsen Ice Shelf

Miles
0 100 200

Kilometres
0 100 200 300

Ice floes punctuate the surface of the Southern Ocean (Photo: Vadim Nefedoff/Shutterstock.com).

(Photo: Vadim Nefedoff/Shutterstock.com).

(Photo: Stephen Lew/Shutterstock.com).

(Photo: Anton Rodionov/Shutterstock.com).

The Union Flag flying at Port Lockroy (Photo: Stewart McPherson).

The territory has no permanently settled population, with neither an elected government of the British Antarctic Territory nor a resident Governor. Instead, the territory is administered through the Foreign and Commonwealth Office through a Commissioner based in London.

The British Antarctic Territory is home to research stations from many countries. The UK maintains five permanent research stations (Halley, Rothera, Signy, Fossil Bluff and Sky Blu), and also staff at historic sites and monuments (such as Port Lockroy). In total, the British stations are staffed by up to 250 people at a time, mainly in the summer.

Port Lockroy is a natural harbour of Wiencke Island, off the Antarctic Peninsula, and was a whaling station from 1911–1931. The tiny Goudier Island in the Port Lockroy harbour was the site of a British research station until 1962. Renovated in 1996, it is now a post office and museum, being the port of call of up to 18 000 Antarctic tourists per year, making it the most visited site in Antarctica. The four staff process about 80 000 pieces of mail each cruise season, from the world's most southerly Royal Mail outpost. Regularly flying the Union Flag and invariably surrounded by penguins, it is understandably popular, and the United Kingdom Antarctic Heritage Trust, which operates the site, uses the proceeds of souvenir and stamp sales to maintain historic sites in the region and gather data on the local wildlife.

Elsewhere in the territory, remains of the devastating South Atlantic whale hunts remain on the geothermally active shores of Deception Island, in the South Shetlands, where a whaling station operated from 1912–1931. Tourists still visit this site today, taking in the remains of this erstwhile industry, but mainly to witness the natural production of hot water by geothermal processes below the sands of the local beach.

The British research station at Port Lockroy (Photo: /Shutterstock.com).

Landscape and Habitats

As most people rightly imagine, Antarctica is a continent of ice, and the British Antarctic Territory is no different. A remarkable 99% of the territory is covered with ice, in some places reaching depths of 5 kilometres. The ice that rests on the continent itself is almost incalculably old, a 1992 palaeoclimatology paper estimating that the freezing of the continent began about 45.5 million years ago (mya), with thick ice sheets forming from about 35 mya. The oldest ice sample recovered to date on Antarctica was drilled in 2015 by Princeton University geochemists. Recovered from a depth of 205 metres, the ice core sample was dated to an astonishing 2.7 million years old, plus or minus 100 000 years!

Here and there, typically close to the coast or where the ice overlies high mountain ranges, the soil and rock of the continent may emerge, either where the ice has melted close to the sea, or in the form of 'nunataks', exposed ridges or peaks that protrude through the ice. The highest parts of the Territory lie within the Eternity mountain range, Mount Hope being the highest peak of all at 3239 metres.

The rocky areas close to the coast and in the few ice-free dry valleys of the continent are where the few flowering plants, mosses and lichens of Antarctica are found.

An iceberg off the Antarctic coast (Photo: abpc/Shutterstock.com).

The stunning coast of the Antarctic Peninsula (Photo: Patrick Poendl/Shutterstock.com).

Penguins gather on the frozen shore (Photo: Anton Ivanov/Shutterstock.com).

(Photo: Aleksei Romanov/Shutterstock.com).

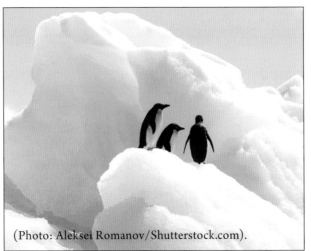
(Photo: Aleksei Romanov/Shutterstock.com).

(Photo: Stephen Lew/Shutterstock.com).

Emperor penguin chicks (Photo: Vlad Silver/Shutterstock.com).

Wildlife

Whilst the number of animals species found on the continent is small, surprising numbers may be present, though almost exclusively along the coasts. Most numerous among them are the penguins, of which five species breed in the territory along with six species of seal. The main reason for the survival of life in the bitter cold of the continent is its rich waters, the upwelling of currents approaching Antarctica bringing huge amounts of nutrients that sustain planktonic life, the base of the polar food chain. These feed krill, the most abundant animal on the planet, which in turn support many organisms, like whales, including the blue whale (the largest animal ever to have lived), not to mention seals, schooling fish, squid, penguins, albatrosses and many other species of birds. The biomass of Antarctic krill is estimated to be 125 to 725 million tonnes, with numbers so large that they can even alter the ocean currents that they live in, causing vital mixing of nutrients through the water column.

The largest entirely terrestrial animal found on Antarctica is a midge, a small insect less than one centimetre in length that has lost its wings. The reason for the loss of its wings is probably associated with the high winds of the continent, which could easily sweep tiny winged animals out to sea and an inevitable death!

Emperor penguins with their chick (Photo: Roger Clark/Shutterstock.com).

The predatory leopard seal (Photo: Dmytro Pylypenko/Shutterstock.com).

The territory's seals are the largest Antarctic predators to venture onto land. The two largest species are the Southern Elephant seal followed by the Leopard seal. The latter species, *Hydrurga leptonyx*, is the top predator in Antarctic waters after the Orca (Killer whale). These seals, which may be over 3 metres in length and weigh over half a tonne, are extremely muscular and make for very capable predators. They feed on a variety of other animals, including fish, squid, most species of penguin and even other seals—including the young of the larger Southern Elephant seal.

With their 2.5 cm canines, they are able to easily grasp prey, a common tactic being to wait under ledges of sea ice for prey to jump into the water before darting at them and snatching them up in their jaws. Surprisingly, the specialised molars of leopard seals also allow them to effectively capture small but nutritious krill, which may make up over 40% of their diet.

These seals have been documented to 'play' with their food, often tossing penguins and seal pups alike into the air. However, it appears that this sort of behaviour is more associated with feeding than it is with any cruel sense of fun. The seals lack the kinds of teeth required to slice through their prey or effectively chew. Like orcas, they may thrash their prey from side to side, beat it against the surface of the water and toss it in the air to break off chunks, splinter bones and make the food easier to consume.

A leopard seal attacking its penguin prey (Photo: Jeremy Holden).

An orca tossing its prey before eating (Photo: Stephen Lew/Shutterstock.com).

The flukes of a diving whale (Photo: Alexey Suloev/Shutterstock.com).

An emerging humpback whale (Photo: Alissa Breit).

The top predator of the British Antarctic is the orca (*Orcinus orca*) or killer whale, technically the world's largest dolphin. These animals hunt in pods of many individuals and have been known to kill the calves of great whales, as well as adult minke, grey whales and smaller sperm whales, chasing them in order to tire them out before drowning them by preventing them from surfacing. They are also known to take most species of seal found in these waters along with all species of penguin. They have demonstrated extreme cunning when hunting, using group tactics to corral their prey into vulnerable positions, or launching themselves onto ice floes to tip unsuspecting animals into their waiting jaws!

The vast quantities of krill in the Antarctic waters make the region one of the best in the world for great whales to feed in prior to their migrations to warmer waters to give birth and rear their young. Species recorded in the waters include blue whales, southern right whales, minke whales, fin whales, sei whales, bowhead whales, sperm whales and humpback whales. It is thus no surprise that, during the whaling heyday, this was the most profitable region within which to hunt. Today, the entire continent of Antarctica is surrounded by an area of 50 million square kilometres designated the Southern Ocean Whale Sanctuary. In it, the International Whaling Commission has banned all types of commercial whaling in a bid to allow whale numbers to recover.

A pair of humpback whales (Photo: Evenfh/Shutterstock.com).

Banks of Antarctic moss and grass (Photo: Stewart McPherson).

Flora

There are very few plants in the British Antarctic Territory, with the majority of the flora consisting of mosses (about 100 species) and liverworts (about 25 species). The mosses, which may grow for only a few weeks each summer, nonetheless form vast cushions and hummocks on account of their considerable age, with individual clumps possibly being centuries old. It is said that the damage caused by footprints can last for decades, so slow is the recovery from the mechanical damage caused by shoes.

There are just two native flowering plants known from the Antarctic Peninsula. These are Antarctic hair grass (*Deschampsia antarctica*) and Antarctic pearlwort (*Colobanthus quitensis*). Also recorded in the territory is the non-native annual blue grass (*Poa annua*). With so many tourists arriving in the territory each year, it is possible that other non-native species may be introduced.

400 lichens and about 750 species of fungi are also recorded. Endemic Antarctic fungi include unusual dung-inhabiting species that colonise the faeces of marine animals that defecate on land. Hundreds of species of algae are also known, including snow algae that can live within the ice, and others that can actually live within sandstone and other sedimentary rocks, growing in between the grains within the stone itself!

Many lichens are recorded from Antarctica (Photo: Stewart McPherson).

The Antarctic pearlwort (Photo: Stewart McPherson).

Protection of the Antarctic Environment

The Antarctic is at once vast and deeply fragile, its living environment subject to brutal cold for much of the year, which limits its ability to adapt to change or to recover from damage. As the single greatest deposit of fresh water on the planet, in the form of its thick and extensive ice caps, it is also one of the most important considerations of long term human survival; significant melting of this stored water would lead to damaging sea level rises that would flood some of the most productive agricultural land on the planet and alter the regular annual weather patterns that we have evolved with.

A variety of treaties protect the entire continent from development, including the 1959 Antarctic Treaty, which designates Antarctica a scientific preserve, guarantees environmental protection, offers freedom of scientific investigation and bans military activity on Antarctica. The 1998 Madrid Protocol bans all mining in Antarctica, formally designating the continent a reserve devoted to peace and science.

Fascinating research published in 2010 revealed that over 230 marine organisms found in Antarctic waters can also be found in the Arctic, the microscopic ones being able to traverse between the north and south poles via deep, cold water currents akin to underwater highways. The continent is connected to the rest of the world in ways that we are clearly yet to understand!

Beneath the Antarctic sea ice (Photo: Hoiseung Jung/Shutterstock.com).

A pair of crabeater seals (Photo: Mariusz Potocki/Shutterstock.com).

Starfish in the waters of the British Antarctic Territory (Photo: Simon Brockington/Shutterstock.com).

The British Indian Ocean Territory is home to some of the most pristine reefs on Earth (Photo: George Duffield).

Population: *circa* 2500 military personnel
Area: 60 sq. km of dry land
Currency: British pound
Capital: N/A
Flag: A series of blue and white lines (the Indian Ocean), with a palm tree rising above the British crown. The Union Flag sits in its canton (top hoist corner).

BRITISH INDIAN OCEAN TERRITORY

The British Indian Ocean Territory is situated about 600 kilometres south of the southernmost islands of the Maldives. The territory covers a vast area of 638 556 square kilometres in the centre of the Indian Ocean, just south of the equator, and though it is the second largest UK Overseas Territory, it overwhelmingly consists of open water only occasionally punctuated by the small atolls that comprise the Chagos Archipelago.

The Chagos Archipelago consists of five atolls (Peros Banhos, Salomon Islands, Great Chagos Bank, Egmont Islands and Diego Garcia), each being more or less a ring of coral island that encircle a shallow lagoon. In total, 55 islands occur across the five atolls, amounting to a combined land area of about 60 square kilometres. Also present in the territory are several submerged atolls, outcrops, banks and seamounts, most of which are marked on official maps and charts. Of these features, Blenheim Reef has a few tiny sandy cays and coral outcrops that may rise above the water surface, especially at low tide.

Atolls are some of the richest marine sites of tropical seas. They develop when coral grows atop the rim of an extinct volcano that has eroded away or submerged under its own weight. As the volcano subsides, the coral covering its rim grows upward, often accumulating coralline limestone at the same rate at which the volcano is submerging. Dish-shaped lagoons typically develop in the centre, with thick layers of sand building up as a result of erosion of the reef and slower currents within the enclosed area, leading to sediment being deposited. Over millions of years, broad fringing coral reefs may form around shallow lagoons, sitting atop layers of limestone kilometres thick above the original volcanic peak. The shallow waters and white, reflective sand beneath account for the brilliant turquoise-blue often associated with atolls.

The islands that form above atolls are result from the gradual accumulation of sand and other sediments on top of the shallow reefs. In time, sand banks rise above the surface of the sea, allowing plants and animals to colonise them. The binding of sand by plant roots can stabilise these banks and even increase the rate at which accumulation of material occurs (this is one of the reasons why deforestation and vegetation removal at coastal areas can lead to serious coastal erosion), but storm surges and unusual tidal events can alter the surface of such islands often, sometimes significantly. Reflecting this formation process, the islands of all atolls consist of flat, low-lying terrain. The highest point across the Chagos Archipelago consists of dune-like rises just 6 m above sea level!

The Archipelago was first documented by fishermen from the Maldives and references to unnamed islands in the Indian Ocean were made by Turkish traders in the 14th century, and later by Portuguese explorers; the first documented visit came in 1513 when nobleman Afonso de Albuquerque encountered Peros Banhos. Claimed by the French in the mid-1700s, the territory was ceded to Britain with the fall of Napoléon Bonaparte and administered from Mauritius. It was designated the British Indian Ocean Territory in 1965.

British Indian Ocean Territory

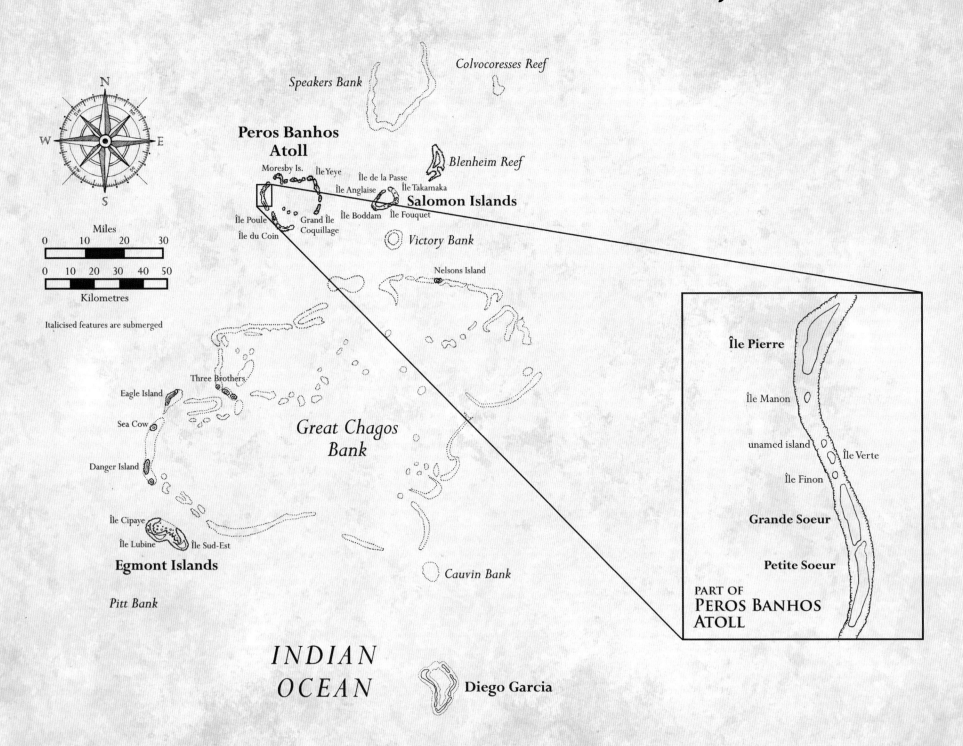

Colvocoresses Reef

Speakers Bank

Peros Banhos Atoll

Moresby Is. Île Yeye

Blenheim Reef

Île de la Passe

Île Anglaise   Île Takamaka

Salomon Islands

Île Poule   Île Boddam   Île Fouquet

Grand Île
Coquillage

Île du Coin

Victory Bank

Nelsons Island

N
W   E
S

Miles
0   10   20   30

0   10 20 30 40 50
Kilometres

Italicised features are submerged

Three Brothers

Eagle Island

Sea Cow

*Great Chagos
Bank*

Danger Island

Île Cipaye

Île Lubine   Île Sud-Est

Egmont Islands

Pitt Bank

Cauvin Bank

*INDIAN
OCEAN*   Diego Garcia

Île Pierre

Île Manon

unamed island   Île Verte

Île Finon

Grande Soeur

Petite Soeur

PART OF
PEROS BANHOS
ATOLL

Atolls comprise virtually all land in the territory (Photo: George Duffield).

Landscape and Habitats

The numerous islands of the British Indian Ocean Territory range in size from just a few square metres to 27.19 square kilometres in the case of the largest atoll, Diego Garcia. All are composed of coralline limestone variably overlaid by sand and, in some cases, forest. The extensive coastline of the islands mean that the littoral (beach) zone is an important habitat, as are the native forests that remain.

Historic clearing of many of the islands to make way for coconut plantations, coupled with the introduction of pest species like rats, has seen biodiversity crash at affected sites. However, on those islands that retain their original hardwood forest cover and remain pest free, the environment could not be more different.

Islands like the strictly protected Île de la Passe and Petite Île Bois Mangue are covered in thick forests of *Barringtonia* and other salt tolerant trees, with an understorey thick with ferns. Moreover, the absence of rats means that the populations of seabirds thrive on the forest floor as in the trees. Given their extreme remoteness, there are no native terrestrial mammals or reptiles on the islands. Instead, they are ruled by birds and crabs. Initiatives to clear islands of rats have begun; after being initially cleared of rats in 2016, the Île Vache Marine was formally declared rat-free in 2017.

Crystal clear waters surround the islands (Photo: Jon Slayer).

Palms on the coast of Île du Coin (Photo: Stewart McPherson).

An adult coconut crab. Individuals may be very colourful, as in this case (Photo: Stewart McPherson).

A coconut crab claw (Photo: Stewart McPherson).

A coconut crab feeding (Photo: Stewart McPherson).

A coconut crab burrow (Photo: Stewart McPherson).

A strawberry hermit crab (Photo: Stewart McPherson).

A crab feeding on the shore (Photo: Simon Vacher).

A land crab on Peros Banhos (Photo: Stewart McPherson)

Wildlife

With the exception of three or four small invertebrates, there is no endemic animal or plant life recorded in the territory. This is because the low-lying islands have been inundated by the sea on a number of occasions—sometimes by severe weather events, or for entire geological periods amounting to thousands of years—before being re-recolonised. As a result, endemic terrestrial species have been prevented from evolving except in rapidly reproducing invertebrates which may produce many generations each year.

Terrestrial animals present on the islands are thus those that most easily colonise island habitats, namely crabs, whose larval stages are planktonic and may easily drift to new habitats, and birds, capable of flying over long distances or, as sometimes occurs, being blown off course to new habitats.

The shorelines are dominated by shore crabs (*Grapsus tenicrustatus*), while the sandy stretches of beach are the domain of ghost crabs (*Ocypode ceratophthalma*). Several species of crab occur within the forests, including the small *Ocypode cordimanus* and a much larger true land crab, the "warrior crab" *Cardisoma carnifex*. The latter live in burrows and only return to the ocean to release their eggs. The most common land crabs are strawberry hermit crabs (*Coenobita perlatus*), which get their name from their mostly bright orangey red colouration punctuated by tiny, pale pimples on the carapace, not unlike the seeds of a strawberry.

The most impressive crab of all, however, is the coconut crab (*Birgus latro*)—the largest of all land crabs and the largest terrestrial invertebrate alive today! Their legs may span 90 cm and the largest individuals weigh up to 4 kg. These incredible animals use their powerful claws to tear open coconuts so that they can consume the nutritious flesh within.

A ghost crab with its unusual, stalked eyes (Photo: Stewart McPherson).

A colourful heliotrope moth (Photo: Stewart McPherson).

The number of bird species is even greater than the number of crabs. To date 127 species of bird have been recorded across the territory, 18 of which form large breeding colonies of at least 250 000 pairs that are of international importance owing to significant declines elsewhere. Species like white terns (*Gygis alba*), bridled terns (*Sterna anaethetus*), brown noddies (*Anous stolidus*) and lesser noddies (*Anous tenuirostris*) flutter continually amongst the hardwood trees of the rat-free islands, and in some places the branches and forest canopy are festooned with hundreds of nests of red-footed boobies (*Sula sula*). Other nesting birds include striated herons (*Butorides striatus*), red-tailed tropicbirds (*Phaethon rubricauda*) and Audubon's shearwater (*Puffinus iherminierii*).

Many of the islands across the Territory are important nesting sites for hawksbill (*Eretymochelys imbricata*) and green sea turtles (*Chelonia mydas*). Roughly 300–700 hawksbills and 400–800 green turtles are estimated to nest annually across the archipelago. In many corners of the globe, rats have been observed eating turtle eggs and hatchlings, especially when other food sources are scarce. It seems possible therefore, that in addition to benefiting bird life, the removal of rats may also enable the numbers of turtles to increase. This would be a significant conservation achievement considering that both turtle species are endangered and the global population of both is sadly in decline.

Many of the islands of the British Indian Ocean Territory are home to large populations of the sooty terns (*Onychoprion fuscatus*), as shown here (Photo: Jon Slayer).

Terns in flight (Photo: Lisa Strachan/Shutterstock.com).

A brown booby (Photo: Simon Vacher).

The striking face of a red-footed booby (Photo: Don Mammoser/Shutterstock.com).

A red-footed booby (Photo: Don Mammoser/Shutterstock.com).

Native hardwood trees on Île de la Passe (Photo: Stewart McPherson).

Flora

On the few islands free of introduced rats and coconut plantations, the original plant ecosystems of these remote Indian Ocean islands remain in rude health. Although many large tree species are present, none of these are endemic, being species that spread readily along ocean currents. In addition to *Barringtonia asiatica*, significant trees include *Calophyllum inophyllum, Cordia subcordata, Guettarda speciosa, Hernandia sonora, Intsia bijuga* and *Pisonia grandis.*

To date, 280 different flowering plants and ferns have been documented in the territory, however only 41 flowering plants and four ferns are native to the islands, the remainder being introduced.

Given the remote nature of the islands, many have not been properly surveyed. As recently as 2010, mangrove forests were discovered on Moresby Island in the north of the Peros Banhos atoll, along with peat swamps which rarely occur on limestone islands.

Mangroves are severely threatened across the world owing to loss of coastal land to human development, while peat swamps are drained and cleared by burning to clear land for oil palm plantations, highlighting the importance of maintaining these fragile islands in as pristine a state as possible.

Scaevola growing close to the shore (Photo: Stewart McPherson).

Bird's nest ferns in the understorey (Photo: Stewart McPherson).

Marine Environment

The waters of the British Indian Ocean Territory are home to spectacular coral reefs made up of corals of every conceivable kind. With some of the least polluted marine conditions on the planet and exceptionally clear waters that allow light to penetrate deeply, diving here is like being in an aquarium. Protected and isolated, the reefs here remain richly populated with little evidence of the destruction caused elsewhere by destructive fishing practices like bomb fishing, cyanide fishing and dredging.

Several reef species occur nowhere else on Earth. One of the most common is the endemic Chagos anemone fish (*Amphiprion chagosensis*), while the Chagos brain coral (*Ctenella chagius*) is also only found in these waters, forming perfect globes with a strangely patterned surface.

Other species that may also be endemic to the waters of the territory include the Chagos dottyback (*Chlidichthys chagosensis*), a wormfish (*Paragunnellichthys fehlmani*), two gobies (*Trimmatom offucius* and *Trimma dalerocheila*), the nymph's cowrie (*Erronea nymphae*) and two margin shells (*Prunum chagosi* and *Marginella henrikasi*).

Detail of a coral on a fringing reef (Photo: Rohan Holt).

A diverse assemblage of corals are recorded from the territory (Photo: Rohan Holt).

A young grey reef shark (Photo: Jon Slayer).

In total, the reefs of the archipelago cover approximately 4000 square kilometres, supporting six times the number of fish found on any other reefs found in the Indian Ocean. The Great Chagos Bank, named after the archipelago, is actually the world's largest coral atoll!

The territory has some of the most biodiverse waters on the planet, with over 300 species of stony coral, 855 species of fish and 355 species of molluscs recorded. In April 2010, a Marine Protected Area banning all fishing and resource extraction activities was declared following years of lobbying by scientists, conservationists and more than 275,000 signatories.

The reefs are not immune to external influences, and a warming trend in the world's oceans resulting from climate change threatens the long term health of all reefs. Following a widespread El Niño event in 1998, and again in 2017, extreme water temperatures led to bleaching and coral death that affected up to 90% of the coral in the territory. However, the otherwise excellent conditions of the reef allowed the ecosystem to almost recover after the 1998 event, whilst reefs elsewhere have hardly recovered, if at all. Insulation of the Chagos reefs from human pressures has been vital to the reefs' ability to recover. For now, they continue to seed the water with fertilised eggs during annual spawnings, acting as a reservoir of much needed young corals for the damaged reefs of the surrounding continental coastlines.

A pair of grunts (Photo: Rohan Holt).

A pair of anemone fish (Photo: Rohan Holt).

The gaping mouth of a giant clam (Photo: Rohan Holt).

A large anemone on the reef (Photo: Rohan Holt).

A gorgonian fan coral on the reef (Photo: Rohan Holt).

Sunset on Pitcairn Island (Photo: Stewart McPherson).

Population: 50 (2018)
Area: 48.7 sq. km of dry land
Currency: New Zealand dollar
Capital: Adamstown
Flag: A Blue Ensign bearing the Pitcairn Islands coat of arms, which features both the anchor and bible of the HMAV Bounty.

PITCAIRN ISLANDS

The Pitcairn Islands are a group of four small islands that lie almost midway between New Zealand and South America in the South Pacific Ocean, just south of the Tropic of Capricorn. They are 2150 km from Tahiti, 2080 km from Easter Island and over 5000 km (approximately the distance from London to New York) away from both New Zealand and South America, the nearest large land masses.

The territory comprises the islands of Ducie, Henderson, Oeno and Pitcairn, which are spread across 650 kilometres of the South Pacific. Henderson is a raised coral atoll (43 sq. km in area), whereas Pitcairn is a rugged volcanic outcrop (4.5 sq. km) and Oeno and Ducie are small, low-lying coral atolls with dry land areas of just 0.7 and 0.5 sq. km respectively. Ducie is the southernmost atoll in the world and the easternmost island of the Indo-Pacific biogeographical province. Whilst all the islands are the visible tops of separate submarine seamounts, Pitcairn Island is the youngest of the group, at around 0.75–1 million years old, and it harbours varied terrain that rises up to 347 m in elevation. In contrast, Henderson, Oeno and Ducie are much older (8-16 million years old) and all have relatively flat topography. The Pitcairn Islands form the UK's only Overseas Territory in the Pacific.

The first European explorer to reach the island group was the Portuguese mariner Pedro Fernandes de Queirós, who sighted Henderson and Ducie Islands in 1606 whilst leading a Spanish expedition. De Queirós named the former San Juan Bautista. In 1767, the crew of the British sloop HMS *Swallow*, commanded by Captain Philip Carteret, reported Pitcairn Island and named it after fifteen-year-old Midshipman Robert Pitcairn, who was the first aboard to sight it. Captain James Henderson, of the British East India Company ship *Hercules*, rediscovered Henderson Island in January 1819, giving it his own name. Captain Henderson was also the first European to sight tiny Oeno in June 1819, but the island was not named until 1824 when Captain George Worth aboard the American whaler *Oeno* named the atoll after his ship.

Although all four islands were uninhabited at the time of European arrival, it is now recognised that Henderson, Pitcairn—and Mangareva, 400 km to the northwest—were inhabited by Polynesian settlers for some centuries prior to their discovery by Europeans. While Mangareva never ceased to be inhabited, Henderson and Pitcairn are likely to have been populated at least into the 15th century. Numerous human artefacts, carvings and skeletal remains have been found on Pitcairn and Henderson and analyses of these artefacts support this belief. While no evidence of Polynesian presence survives on Oeno or Ducie, which are unlikely to have been settled owing to lack of ample fresh water and food, it is probable that both were visited by the Polynesian traffic that is known to have connected Pitcairn and Easter Island centuries ago.

Pitcairn Islands

Oeno Island

Henderson Island

Ducie Island

Pitcairn Island

PACIFIC OCEAN

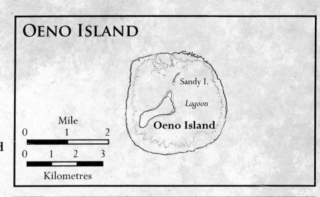

OENO ISLAND

Sandy I.

Lagoon

Oeno Island

Mile
0   1   2

0   1   2   3
Kilometres

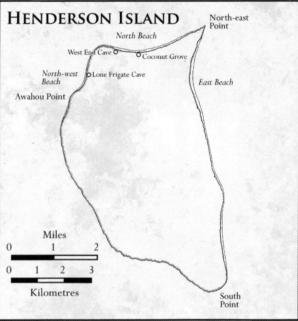

HENDERSON ISLAND

North-east Point

North Beach

West End Cave   Coconut Grove

North-west Beach   Lone Frigate Cave

East Beach

Awahou Point

Miles
0   1   2

0   1   2   3
Kilometres

South Point

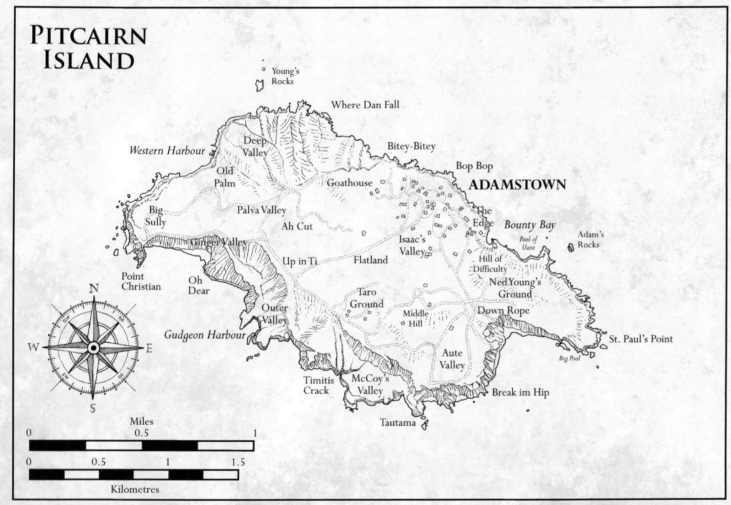

PITCAIRN ISLAND

Young's Rocks

Where Dan Fall

Bitey-Bitey

Deep Valley

Western Harbour

Bop Bop

ADAMSTOWN

Old Palm

Goathouse

Big Sully

Palva Valley

The Edge

Bounty Bay

Ah Cut

Pool of Uara

Adam's Rocks

Ginger Valley

Isaac's Valley

Point Christian

Up in Ti

Flatland

Hill of Difficulty

Oh Dear

Ned Young's Ground

Outer Valley

Taro Ground

Down Rope

Gudgeon Harbour

Middle Hill

St. Paul's Point

Big Pool

Aute Valley

Timitis Crack

McCoy's Valley

Break im Hip

Tautama

N
W   E
S

Miles
0   0.5   1

0   0.5   1   1.5
Kilometres

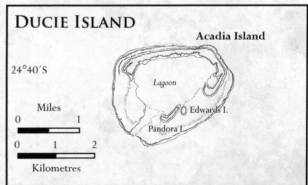

DUCIE ISLAND

Acadia Island

24°40'S

Lagoon

Edwards I.

Pandora I.

Miles
0   1

0   1   2
Kilometres

The Mutiny on the *Bounty*

Pitcairn Island is the only island in this group to have a permanent population. It was populated by the ancestors of today's inhabitants in one of the most frequently recounted events in British maritime history, the Mutiny on the HMAV *Bounty*, an armed vessel captained by 33 year old Lieutenant William Bligh on a mission to transport breadfruit trees from Tahiti to the West Indies to supply slaves with a cheap and plentiful food.

Arriving in Tahiti in late October 1788, the crew was overwhelmed by the welcoming nature of the people and their idyllic island life. During the five months spent on the island preparing their cargo of 1015 breadfruit plants, the crew formed relationships with the island's women, the first mate (and friend of Captain Bligh) Christian Fletcher marrying Maimiti, a Tahitian woman. Following their April departure, cruel and callous behaviour by the captain is alleged to have quickly led to discontent amongst the crew.

On 28 April, 24 days after setting off, Christian led a mutiny against Captain Bligh, setting him and most of his loyal crew adrift in a launch, Christian led the *Bounty* back to Tahiti and soon onwards to Pitcairn. Finding the island 300 km west of where the Royal Navy's coordinates reported it to be, Christian recognised it as an excellent hiding place. The mutineers marooned themselves there in January 1790 by setting fire to the *Bounty*.

The *Bounty* arriving in Tahiti (John Hagan/Pitcairn Islands Study Centre).

A depiction of the mutiny on the *Bounty* (John Hagan/Pitcairn Islands Study Centre).

The burning of the *Bounty* off Pitcairn (John Hagan/Pitcairn Islands Study Centre).

Most residents are descendants of the mutineers (Photo: Stewart McPherson).

Adamstown

Named after John Adams, the last surviving mutineer, the hamlet of Adamstown is the second smallest capital in the world and the capital of the world's smallest nation, being the place where the entire population of 50 people live and work. It is one of the most isolated settlements on Earth. Official buildings include the community hall, several offices of the Government and Mayor, the treasury office, a post office, a church and a school. The British Government has an agreement with New Zealand that sees the latter policing the island, providing a medic, a teacher and a social worker. The Governor of Pitcairn is not stationed on the island, but in New Zealand, though a Foreign Office representative is often present. The local Government is headed by a democratically elected mayor and an Island Council.

The islanders grow a wide variety of fruits and vegetables around the island—including passionfruit, bananas, papayas, sugar cane, coconuts and breadfruit—and some also rear chickens for their eggs. Additional protein is sourced from the ocean, with fish forming a major part of the local diet. Honey production and handicraft making also earn valuable export revenue. Adamstown is rich with artefacts from the *Bounty* including canons, anchors, a bible and ship's bell. Each year, on January 23rd, the population commemorate the burning of the *Bounty* by setting light to an effigy of the tall ship.

A relict from the *Bounty* (Photo: Stewart McPherson).

Re-enacting the burning of the *Bounty* (Photo: Stewart McPherson).

Landscape and Habitats

The Pitcairn Islands were formed as the result of magma upwelling through a volcanic hotspot in the Pacific known as the Pitcairn Hotspot. They are the southeasternmost extension of the French Polynesia Tuamotu Archipelago, the largest chain of atolls in the world! While the uninhabitable Oeno and Ducie Islands are both atolls consisting of five and four islets respectively, Pitcairn and Henderson Islands are rather different.

Henderson was once an atoll, but a period of geological activity saw the atoll raised to form an uplifted coral island composed of reef rubble, limestone and eroded material. Its coasts mainly consist of steep 15 metre high cliffs, making access difficult, but the interior is flat and covered in vegetation up to five metres tall and rich with wildlife. A single source of fresh water is known and historic human artefacts have been found on the island.

Pitcairn is much smaller than Henderson and of volcanic origin. Access is similarly limited because of its steep cliffs, but boats can land at the natural harbour of Bounty Bay. Although it is home to fewer endemic species than Henderson, its soils are deeper and richer, allowing its populace to grow fruit and vegetables for survival. The islands have a tropical climate with average temperatures of about 24 °C during the summer period to 19°C in winter when rainfall may increase significantly, July being the wettest month.

A view from the southeast outcrop across the island (note the triangular cave below the peak in the north of the island) (Photo: Stewart McPherson).

The interior of Henderson Island is pristine and inaccessible (Photo: Sue O'Keefe).

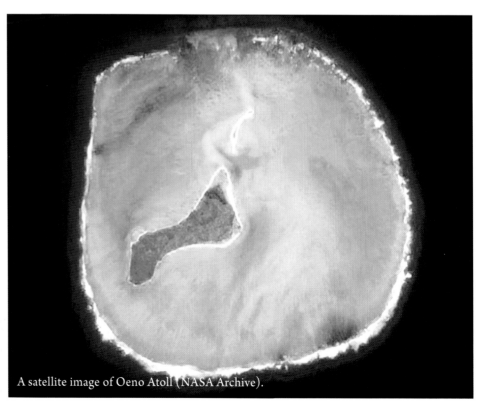

A satellite image of Oeno Atoll (NASA Archive).

A Pitcairn island reed warbler (Photo: Sue O'Keefe).

A masked booby on Henderson island (Photo: Stewart McPherson).

The population of white terns found across the Pitcairn Islands represents an endemic subspecies (*Gygis alba leucopes*). Large numbers of this beautiful bird nest on Henderson Island (Photo: Simon Vacher).

Wildlife

Of all the four islands, Pitcairn's wildlife has been the most impacted by long term human disturbance, introduced pests and habitat competitors. A total of 43 bird species have been recorded in the territory, of which 20 species breed on the islands. Of these, 16 are recorded from Henderson, 13 on Ducie, 12 on Oeno and six on Pitcairn.

Only one bird is endemic to Pitcairn itself, namely the Pitcairn Reed Warbler (*Acrocephalus vaughani*) a songbird that the islanders refer to simply as a "sparrow" (a name probably given to it by the original mutineers). As of 2008, the bird has been afforded endangered status on account of its small range and declining population.

Non-endemic birds that breed on the island include white terns (*Gygis alba*), red-tailed tropicbirds (*Phaethon rubricauda*) and noddies, but it is known that other species used to breed on the island, including gannets, as evidenced by places named after historic bird colonies, such as Gannets' Ridge.

The island includes a number of other interesting animals, including beach crabs with incredible camouflage that matches the multicoloured grains of sand; as well as a giant tortoise, "Mrs T", introduced from the Galapagos between 1937–1951, who is believed to be over a century old.

The beautiful red-tailed tropicbird (*Phaethon rubricauda*) breeds on both Oeno and Ducie Islands (Photo: Mike Pienkowski).

A camouflaged beach crab (Photo: Stewart McPherson).

The century old "Mrs T" (Photo: Sue O'Keefe).

The coast of Henderson island (Photo: Stewart McPherson).

Henderson Island offers an altogether different range of habitats. It is the last example in the Pacific of a raised coral atoll with an intact ecosystem and boasts four endemic land bird species—the Henderson fruit dove, Henderson lorikeet, Henderson reed warbler and the flightless Henderson crake. Three other species, the Henderson ground dove, the Henderson imperial pigeon and the Henderson archaic pigeon, were endemic to the island, but became extinct when Polynesians arrived during the 11th century.

At least nine species of non-endemic seabird are thought to breed on Henderson, including the globally endangered Henderson petrel. This bird used to occur on Ducie atoll, but was last recorded there in 1922, after which the last remaining nests were destroyed by invasive rats. While Ducie and Oeno have now been cleared of rats, they sadly remain on Henderson Island and have decimated some of the bird populations there. Over £1.5 million was spent on eradicating them from Henderson in 2011. Unfortunately, surviving rats were recorded in 2012, demonstrating that this effort failed, perhaps because the effort was not sustained over a longer period.

The island is the easternmost limit of the giant Coconut Crab, and while its invertebrate population is not well studied, about a third of the island's known non-marine gastropods (snails and slugs) and insects are thought to be endemic.

A young hermit crab at rest on a tree (Photo: Stewart McPherson).

The unique Henderson fruit dove (*Ptilinopus insularis*) is also known as scarlet-capped fruit dove (Photo: Simon Vacher).

The Henderson reed warbler (*Acrocephalus taiti*) is another bird found nowhere else other than Henderson Island (Photo: Sue O'Keefe).

The Henderson crake (*Porzana atra*) occurs nowhere else on Earth (Photo: Mike Pienkowski).

The endemic Henderson lorikeet (*Vini stepheni*) (Photo: Simon Vacher).

The Henderson petrel (*Pterodroma atrata*) roams far and wide over the Pacific but is known to breed only on Henderson Island (Photo: Stewart McPherson).

The yellow fatu is the national flower of Pitcairn (Photo: Stewart McPherson).

Flora

Many of Pitcairn's endemic plants are known from just a handful of individuals. The endemic red berry (*Coprosma benefica*) had a population of only 11 individuals before on-island propagation boosted its numbers; while the giant nehe fern (*Angiopteris chauliodonta*) is restricted to small and fragmented populations. Pitcairn's national flower, the yellow fatu (*Abutilon pitcairnense*) was actually thought to be extinct, but a single specimen was found in the wild by islander Carol Warren in 2003. Cuttings from this plant were rooted and then transferred to Trinity College Botanic Gardens, Dublin, establishing reserve populations across Europe. The timing of this was very fortunate since a landslide destroyed the only wild plant in January 2005.

A wide variety of introduced plants occur on Pitcairn, including the plant that shaped the island's history, the breadfruit (*Artocarpus altilis*). This valuable food plant may have been introduced from Tahiti by the mutineers of the *Bounty*, or perhaps by the first Polynesian settlers. Its large fruits are abundant and provide a good source of carbohydrate. Like the potato, it can be boiled, fried, formed into patties or curried, making it highly versatile.

Henderson Island, whose extensive forest and scrub has a largely intact floral assemblage, is home to about 50 native plant species, ten of which are endemic to the island.

The giant nehe fern is endemic to Pitcairn (Photo: Stewart McPherson).

The breadfruit is an integral part of Pitcairn life (Photo: Stewart McPherson).

Marine Environment

The underwater world of the Pitcairn Islands is astounding and, at over 800 000 sq. km of ocean, represents an area more than three times larger than the surface area of the entire United Kingdom. The remote location and low population density of the islands have preserved the waters of the territory and protected them from unsustainable levels of fishing.

The number of marine plant and animal species recorded from the waters of the territory stands at over 1275. It includes the world's deepest living plant, a species of encrusting coralline alga found at a depth of 312m off Ducie. The cool waters restrict the variety of corals, but several of those species present occur at greater depths than in many other parts of the Pacific on account of the exceptional clarity of the water. The ecosystem of hard and soft corals is home to many unique species, including the gastropod *Fusinus galatheae bountyi*, named after HMAV *Bounty*. Species endemic to particular islands include the Pitcairn sandlance (*Ammodytoides leptus*) and the many-spined butterflyfish (*Hemitaurichthys multispinosus*), known only from Pitcairn Island; a nudibranch (*Bornella irvingi*), known only from the waters of Ducie Island; and the Henderson triplefin (*Enneapterygius ornatus*) and the Henderson squirrelfish (*Sargocentron megalops*) are known only from the waters of Henderson Island.

The exquisite waters that surround Henderson Island support extensive coral reefs (Photo: Sue O'Keefe).

Double saddled butterfly fish (Photo: RA Irving).

Smith's butterfly fish, an endemic species (Photo: RA Irving).

A view across Bermuda from Gibb's Hill Lighthouse (Photo: Stewart McPherson).

Population: 65 331 (2016)
Area: 53.7 sq. km of dry land
Currency: Bermudian dollar
Capital: Hamilton
Flag: A Red Ensign bearing the Bermuda coat of arms—lion of England and a shield bearing the wrecked ship *Sea Venture*, whose foundering led to first settlement.

BERMUDA

Bermuda is located in the western North Atlantic, approximately 1040 kilometres east of Cape Hatteras, North Carolina, the nearest point of land on any continental land mass. Bermuda is actually the oldest of the UK's Overseas Territories and also the most populous. The Territory consists of a 'mainland'—comprised of eight islands that are now connected by bridges and causeways—and approximately 193 smaller islands and islets that lie in shallow lagoons formed by the main islands or are scattered close by. Fifty six of the smaller islands are inhabited or have been settled previously.

The islands of Bermuda are the summit region of a mid-Atlantic seamount that rises from a depth of 4000 metres. In the past, when global sea levels were higher, the submerged summit of the Bermudian seamount was encrusted with coral that formed a thick cap of limestone. The geologically recent decline in sea level exposed some of the limestone deposits in the form of the Bermudian islands seen today. As a result, all of the islands of Bermuda are very flat and the highest point of land—Town Hill, on the mainland—rises to just 78 m. Most of the rest of the islands consist of low plains and undulating rises. Bermuda lies directly in the path of the warm waters of the Gulf Stream. The surrounding area of submerged seamount covers about 1000 sq. km, and bears the northernmost tropical coral reefs in the world.

The first known European explorer to reach Bermuda was Spanish captain Juan de Bermúdez, who arrived aboard the vessel La Garza in 1503. The Italian-born historian of Spain, Peter Martyr d'Anghiera, depicted an island called "La Bermuda" in his 1511 book *Legatio Babylonica*, which records Spanish discoveries during the Age of Exploration, including those of the Bermúdez expedition. Juan de Bermúdez returned to his namesake island in 1515, this time with the chronicler Gonzalo Fernández de Oviedo y Valdés. Oviedo's account of this visit, published in 1526, records that they made no attempt to land on account of the weather. Although the Spanish declared Bermuda part of their empire, the island was never colonised until a ship, the *Sea Venture*—captained by Admiral Sir George Somers on a voyage from Plymouth to Jamestown, Virginia—was deliberately run onto the island's reef to prevent the ship from sinking in a storm in 1609. In 1612, a Royal Charter was extended to include Bermuda as an extension of the British Colony of Virginia and a party of 60 settlers was sent to settle the colony. Bermuda formally became a Crown Colony in 1614.

Bermuda is unique amongst the UK Overseas Territories in that virtually the entire surface of the mainland is suburban. St. George's Town, the first settlement on the islands, was the capital until 1815, when most government offices moved to the new capital, Hamilton, thereby providing a more centrally-located seat of governance.

Bermuda

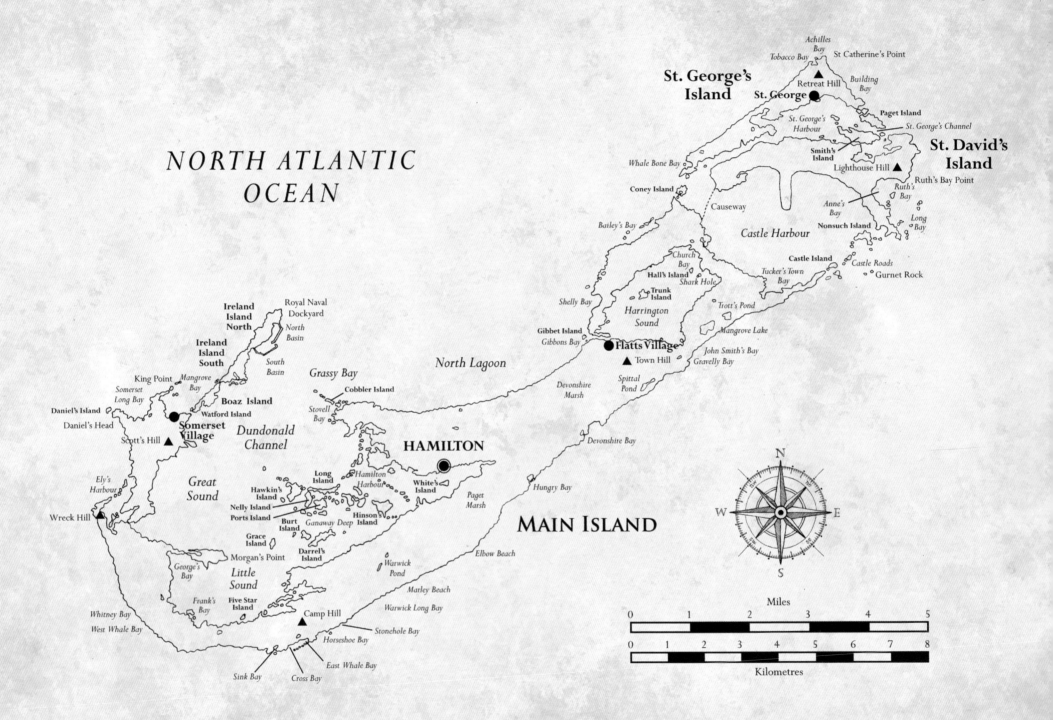

NORTH ATLANTIC OCEAN

Achilles Bay
Tobacco Bay
St Catherine's Point

St. George's Island
Retreat Hill ▲
St. George ●
Building Bay

Paget Island

St. George's Harbour
St. George's Channel

St. David's Island

Whale Bone Bay
Smith's Island
Lighthouse Hill ▲

Ruth's Bay
Ruth's Bay Point

Coney Island
Causeway
Anne's Bay
Long Bay

Bailey's Bay
Nonsuch Island

Castle Harbour

Castle Island
Castle Roads

Church Bay
Tucker's Town Bay
Gurnet Rock

Hall's Island
Shark Hole

Trott's Pond

Trunk Island

Shelly Bay
Harrington Sound
Mangrove Lake

Gibbet Island
Gibbons Bay
John Smith's Bay
Gravelly Bay

Flatts Village ●
Town Hill ▲

North Lagoon

Devonshire Marsh

Spittal Pond

Ireland Island North

Royal Naval Dockyard
North Basin

Ireland Island South

South Basin
Grassy Bay

King Point
Mangrove Bay

Somerset Long Bay

Boaz Island
Watford Island

Cobbler Island

Stovell Bay

Daniel's Island

Daniel's Head

Somerset Village ●

Scott's Hill ▲

Dundonald Channel

HAMILTON ◉

Hamilton Harbour

White's Island

Long Island

Ely's Harbour

Great Sound

Hawkin's Island

Nelly Island
Ports Island

Paget Marsh

Hungry Bay

Wreck Hill ▲

Burt Island
Ganaway Deep

Hinson's Island

Grace Island

Darrel's Island

Morgan's Point

George's Bay

Little Sound

Warwick Pond

Devonshire Bay

MAIN ISLAND

Frank's Bay

Five Star Island

Camp Hill ▲

Elbow Beach

Whitney Bay

West Whale Bay

Stonehole Bay

Marley Beach
Warwick Long Bay

Horseshoe Bay
East Whale Bay

Sink Bay
Cross Bay

N
W E
S

Miles
0 1 2 3 4 5

0 1 2 3 4 5 6 7 8
Kilometres

Historic Carter House with its water-collecting roof (Photo: Stewart McPherson).

St. George's Town

Settled in 1612, St. George's Town is the former capital of Bermuda and the oldest continuously inhabited English town in the New World. The town was designated a UNESCO World Heritage Site in 2000 in recognition of its historic centre and numerous fortifications. Its traditional dwellings are built out of stone to be robust against hurricanes, while the roofs of most buildings are grooved and specifically designed to collect vital fresh water.

While Bermuda officially remained loyal to the Crown during the American War of Independence, the Government powder magazine at St. George's was broken open by American sympathisers and 100 barrels of gunpowder stolen and shipped to George Washington's army. The shipment arrived at a critical time. It is said that this act enabled Washington to gain a series of victories that tipped the balance of the conflict in his favour.

Landscape and Habitats

The high population density means that none of Bermuda's terrestrial habitats are pristine; the most remote of the smaller islands and the nearby coral reefs harbour the least disturbed ecosystems in the territory, including salt marshes, caves, freshwater marshes, brackish ponds and mangrove forests. Nevertheless, at least 250 plant and animal species are unique to Bermuda.

Virtually all of Bermuda's mainland is developed (Photo: Stewart McPherson).

Native vegetation on Nonsuch Island (Photo: Stewart McPherson).

The exquisitely beautiful white-tailed tropicbird (*Phaethon lepturus catsbyii*) (Photo: Simon Vacher).

A great kiskadee (*Pitangus sulphuratus*), one of many introduced bird species (Photo: Mike Pienkowski).

The native eastern bluebird (*Sialia sialis*) (Photo: Mike Pienkowski).

A northern cardinal (*Cardinalis cardinalis*). This species was introduced to Bermuda in 1700 (Photo: Mike Pienkowski).

A non-native Jamaican anole (*Anolis Grahami*) with dewlap extended (Photo: Mike Pienkowski).

Wildlife

Since colonisation, the islands of Bermuda have been severely impacted by land clearing, development and introduced predators and pest species. Species now extinct include a tortoise, a woodpecker, a hawk, four species of rail, a crane and a flightless duck and doubtless others that were never documented.

The only native mammals are the islands bats, of which there are five species, none endemic. In fact, the only surviving endemic terrestrial vertebrate in Bermuda is the Bermuda skink (*Plestiodon longirostris*), a critically endangered species mainly found on a few of the small, rocky, outer islands and in a few mainland reserves. The most common lizard on the island is an introduced anole (*Anolis grahami*) which, along with three other introduced anoles, competes with the skink for habitat.

Best known of all the endemic animals is the Bermuda petrel (*Pterodroma cahow*), commonly known as the cahow. This bird is an example of a Lazarus species, so-called because of its apparent return from the dead: adults and eggs of this super-abundant species were taken in their thousands during the 1600s, resulting in the species apparently going extinct in the 1620s. However, in 1935 a bird that struck a local lighthouse and died was identified as a cahow, and a living bird was found injured in 1941.

The Jamaican anole (*Anolis Grahami*) may change colour dramatically and become bright blue (Photo: Alison Copeland).

A cahow chick being weighed (Photo: Stewart McPherson).

Prompted by these sightings of an 'extinct' bird, searches for living cahows were eventually mounted. Finally, in 1951, 18 surviving pairs were found nesting across five rocky islets. The species officially regarded as extinct for well over 300 years was alive and breeding!

The small islets where the cahows had been found were rocky and uninhabited. A couple were little more than outcrops of limestone that rose above the water by just a few metres. All five islands were soon protected, but they were all vulnerable to flooding by hurricanes or storm surges, making it a miracle that the cahows had survived at all.

An ambitious conservation strategy was developed which centred on the idea of translocating cahows from the five small islets where they were found to a much larger island called Nonsuch. This island first had to be cleared of pests and replanted, a process that began in 1963; in the meantime, artificial burrows were built and tested on their few islets to provide more nests and encourage additional laying, leading to a population of 55 by 2001. In 2004, a trial translocation of 14 chicks to Nonsuch took place, with another of 21 chicks in 2005, and a total of 102 by 2008. The chicks were fed and monitored every day until they were successfully fledged, the young birds thereafter departing for their life at sea. In 2008, the first fledglings returned as adults to lay the first natural cahow egg on Nonsuch in 2009!

An artificial nest for cahows (Photo: Stewart McPherson).

An adult cahow in flight (Photo: Brian Patterson).

The efforts to expand the colony have come to be regarded as a complete success and the recovery has progressed well. As of the 2015 season, the global cahow population is thought to number approximately 300, with 111 breeding pairs, 14 of those on Nonsuch island and the remainder on the five original islets.

The success of this endeavour took a concerted effort by a limited number of individuals who made it their life's work to ensure the well being of the cahows, but it was not achieved without difficulties. On more than one occasion the nesting sites were attacked by rats that had swum to them from the mainland, while tropicbirds actively compete for the nest burrows and will kill cahow chicks if unable to locate an unoccupied burrow. The rats were dispatched as soon as they were detected, and vigilant checks are made to ensure that they do not return, while the larger tropicbirds are simply excluded by putting wooden baffles across the burrow entrances to physically prevent them from entering.

The role that offshore islands played in the survival of unique wildlife like the cahow and Bermuda skink cannot be overstated; without them, these animals would now be extinct. However, and against all odds, an 'extinct' species of snail (*Poecilozonites bermudensis*) was recently discovered in an alley of the town of Hamilton, protected from predators by the city's walls!

A tropicbird in an artificial nest (Photo: Stewart McPherson).

The endemic snail rediscovered in Hamilton (Photo: Stewart McPherson).

The endemic Bermuda Skink (*Plestiodon longirostris*) (Photo: Alison Copeland).

The bermudiana, the national flower (Photo: Stewart McPherson).

Flora

Although there are 165 species of plant native to Bermuda, only 12 of them are endemic. The largest of these is the Bermuda juniper (*Juniperus bermudiana*), a tree that used to cover much of the island until it was cut down for use as a building material or firewood and cleared by burning to make way for development.

However, the greatest damage to this species was the introduction of two species of tiny scale insect, which killed over 99% (about eight million trees) of the remaining forest. A small number proved resistant to the pest insects and these are being propagated to slowly repopulate the island with native trees, but only 10% of original coverage has been restored.

Other endemic species include the severely threatened Governor Laffan's fern (*Diplazium laffanianum*), once extinct in nature but being introduced from surviving material from botanic gardens, the Bermuda palmetto (*Sabal bermudana*), Bermuda sedge (*Carex bermudiana*), Bermuda pepper (*Peperomia septentrionalis*), Bermuda olivewood (*Elaeodendron laneanum*), Bermuda bean (*Phaseolus lignosus*), the Bermudiana (*Sisyrinchium bermudiana*), Darrell's Fleabane (*Erigeron darrellianus*), Bermuda shield fern (*Thelypteris bermudiana*) and Bermuda maidenhair fern (*Adiantum bellum*).

The native prickly pear (*Opuntia stricta*) (Photo: Stewart McPherson).

Sea ox-eye (*Borrichia arborescens*) (Photo: Stewart McPherson).

Marine Environment

Bermuda has the northern-most tropical coral reefs and tropical seagrass beds in the Atlantic, as well as the northern-most mangroves in the western Atlantic. The marine environment of Bermuda is home to hundreds of native species, among these are five endemic marine fish species, including the Bermuda anchovy (*Anchoa choerostoma*), Bermuda halfbeak (*Hemiramphus bermudensis*), Bermuda goby (*Lythrypnus mowbrayi*), Bermuda bream (*Diplodus bermudensis*) and the Bermuda tilefish (*Caulolatilus bermudensis*).

It is worth mentioning that the islands are home to other endemic aquatic animals, such as the Bermuda killifish (*Fundulus bermudae*), which is found in freshwater and brackish water ponds and marshes. Sadly it is now known from just seven locations. Another species, the Lover's Lake killifish (*Fundulus relictus*) is known from just three ponds!

Also of interest are the animals that occur only in Bermuda's anchialine caves—these are caves that are landlocked, but connected through rock aquifers to the ocean, meaning that they can be fresh or salty in different parts! Some of the animals from these cave environments are highly specialised, for example the critically endangered Bermuda Cave Shrimp (*Mictocaris halope*), discovered in 1985. They live only in darkness, are completely colourless and have no eyes, navigating and feeding in the caves using their other senses.

A tropical coral reef at North Rock, Bermuda (Photo: Alison Copeland / Department of Environment and Natural Resources).

The endemic Bermuda bream (*Diplodus bermudensis*) (Photo: Department of Environment and Natural Resources).

The endemic Lover's Lake killifish (*Fundulus relictus*) is known from just three ponds on Bermuda. Above is male, below is female. (Photo: Alison Copeland / Department of Environment and Natural Resources).

The rare blue iguana (Photo: Stewart McPherson).

Population: 60 765 (2016)
Area: 264 sq. km of dry land
Currency: Cayman Islands dollar
Capital: George Town, Grand Cayman
Flag: A Blue Ensign bearing the islands' coat of arms—three stars representing the islands, the lion for Britain, and a sea turtle (once very numerous in their waters).

CAYMAN ISLANDS

The Cayman Islands lie 300 kilometres directly south of the Cuban mainland and approximately 730 kilometres east of the Belize-Mexico border on the Yucatan peninsula. The territory consists of three islands that lie on a mostly submarine ridge that extends west from the southern tip of Cuba almost all the way to the Central American region of the North American mainland. The three islands are Grand Cayman, Little Cayman and Cayman Brac. Grand Cayman is by far the largest island in the group, with an area of 196 sq. km and around 95% of the territory's population. The smaller islands, Little Cayman and Cayman Brac both lie to the northeast of Grand Cayman. These two islands are similar in size and consist of narrow, closely situated strips of land angled roughly east to west. Cayman Brac lies 140 km from Grand Cayman, has an area of 38 sq. km and a population of approximately 2100. Little Cayman is the smallest and least developed of the group; it lies around 120 km from Grand Cayman, has an area of 28.5 sq. km and a population of about 170. Little Cayman and Cayman Brac are often called the Sister Islands on account of their similarities and lie just 6 km from one another.

All three Cayman Islands are flat and low-lying. They are composed of coralline limestone and rise noticeably in only a few areas; the highest point on Grand Cayman is a mere 18 m above sea level—at a hill optimistically named "the mountain"—while a plateau on Cayman Brac rises up to 43 m, forming the highest prominence in the territory. The interior of the Cayman Islands is clothed with tropical dry forest and scrub, while much of the coastline is lined with patches of mangrove forest and beautiful beaches. The islands are surrounded by extensive fringing reefs that enclose shallow lagoons and coral gardens, regarded as amongst the most beautiful in all of the Americas.

The first European to reach the Cayman group was Christopher Columbus, during his fourth and final voyage to the New World. On 10 May 1503, Columbus' ship, blown off course, sighted Little Cayman and Cayman Brac, which he named "Las Tortugas"—the turtles. The choice of name is explained by Ferdinand Columbus, Christopher's son, also present on the voyage: "We were in sight of two very small and low islands, full of tortoises [sea turtles], as was all the sea all about, insomuch that they looked like little rocks." Columbus did not land on the islands, but sailed on to his intended destination, Hispaniola. The islands were mostly uninhabited into the 1600s, but are likely to have been settled after the capture of Jamaica in 1655. Formal control of the territory fell to Britain in 1670 and a permanent settlement was established on the islands from 1734. Unlike on most Caribbean islands, there is no archaeological evidence for the presence of any indigenous Americans on any of the Cayman Islands, perhaps because the group was simply too small and too distant from land for them to reach easily.

Cayman Islands

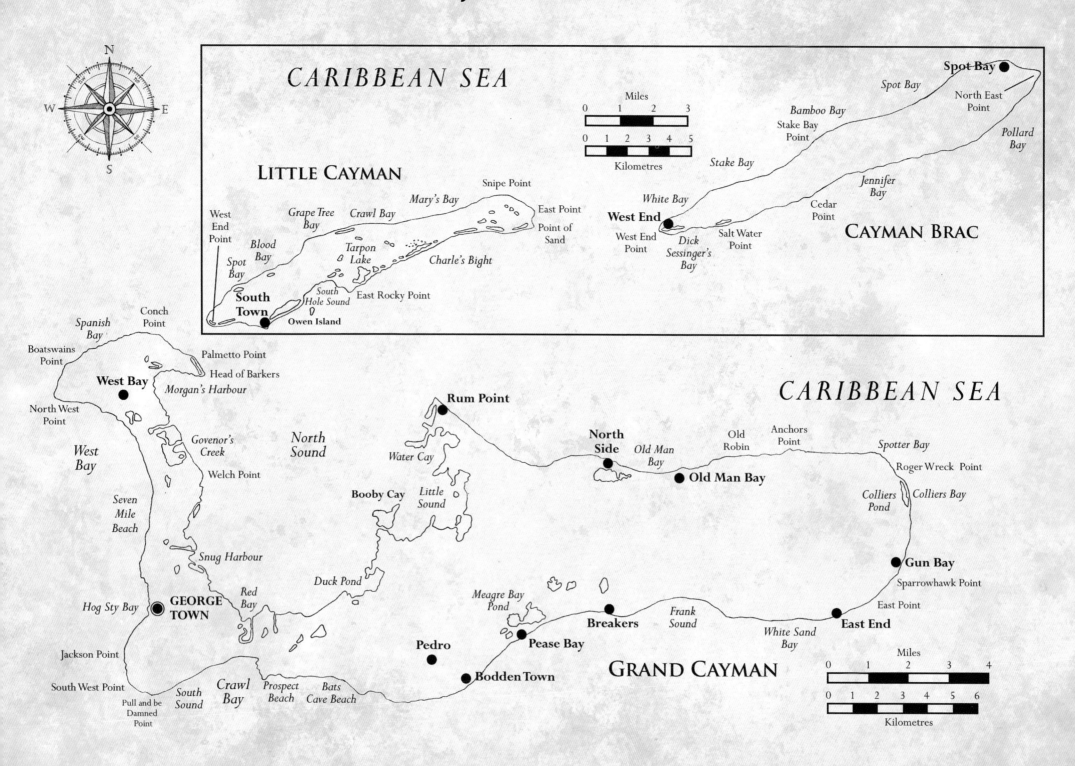

CARIBBEAN SEA

Miles
0 1 2 3

0 1 2 3 4 5
Kilometres

LITTLE CAYMAN

Snipe Point

Mary's Bay

Grape Tree Bay
Crawl Bay
West End Point
Blood Bay
Spot Bay
Tarpon Lake
Charle's Bight
East Point
Point of Sand
South Hole Sound
East Rocky Point
South Town
Owen Island

West End
West End Point
White Bay
Dick Sessinger's Bay
Salt Water Point

CAYMAN BRAC

Spot Bay
Spot Bay
North East Point
Bamboo Bay
Stake Bay Point
Pollard Bay
Stake Bay
Cedar Point
Jennifer Bay

CARIBBEAN SEA

Spanish Bay
Conch Point
Boatswains Point
Palmetto Point
Head of Barkers
West Bay
Morgan's Harbour
North West Point
Govenor's Creek
North Sound
Rum Point
West Bay
Welch Point
Water Cay
North Side
Old Man Bay
Old Robin
Anchors Point
Spotter Bay
Roger Wreck Point
Seven Mile Beach
Booby Cay
Little Sound
Old Man Bay
Colliers Pond
Colliers Bay
Snug Harbour
Duck Pond
Gun Bay
GEORGE TOWN
Red Bay
Meagre Bay Pond
Sparrowhawk Point
Hog Sty Bay
East Point
Breakers
Frank Sound
East End
Jackson Point
Pedro
Pease Bay
White Sand Bay
South West Point
Crawl Bay
Prospect Beach
Bats Cave Beach
Bodden Town
GRAND CAYMAN
Pull and be Damned Point
South Sound

Miles
0 1 2 3 4

0 1 2 3 4 5 6
Kilometres

A native butterfly (Photo: Stewart McPherson).

A red-footed booby (Photo: Stacy Funderburke/Shutterstock.com).

An island pygmy boa (Photo: Stewart McPherson).

Downtown George Town (Photo: Stewart McPherson).

George Town

The city of George Town is the capital of the Cayman islands and the second most populous settlement in the UK Overseas Territories, being home to the majority of people on Grand Cayman. As the main port of entry to the islands, the city is as much a centre of island-wide tourism as it is of government and, of course, banking.

Banking is the most significant area of commerce in the Cayman islands. With over 500 banking companies established in the town, as well as branches of most of the 50 largest banks in the world present, this sector amounts to 55% of the total economy, accounting for nearly 40% of all jobs and almost half of government revenue. This is because the islands have never levied income tax, capital gains tax or any wealth tax, seeing this small city developing into one of the world's top financial hubs.

The Caymans are known for their unspoiled beaches and spectacular reefs. As a result many cruise ships call into George Town's harbour during the week, with passengers coming ashore to shop and dine in the vibrant central district, as well as to go on various tours, usually to see underwater life by way of scuba diving, snorkelling, boat trips and even a submarine! Local tourism is aimed at the luxury end of the spectrum, with many high end hotels and resorts established around the city as well as across the islands.

Colourful beach houses (Photo: Sandarina/Shutterstock.com).

An aerial view of Grand Cayman (Photo: Richard Whitcomb/Shutterstock.com).

Landscape and Habitats

Unlike some of the older territories, like Bermuda, the Cayman islands remain relatively forested, particularly the small islands of Little Cayman and Cayman Brac, which are far less developed and still largely covered with natural vegetation. Even so, Grand Cayman still has extensive natural vegetation cover, including the Mastic Reserve, a large old growth seasonally wet forest named after an endemic variety of mastic tree. The forests are very rich as they have not been flood by seawater for over two million years, unlike the remaining territory of the islands, and contain a broad variety of drought tolerant species including bromeliads and climbing cacti.

Mangroves occupy the wetlands at the centre of Grand Cayman, but are far less frequently visited. The mangroves cover around 30% of the centre of the island, or an area of approximately 12 km by 7 km, known as the Central Mangrove Wetland. Few visitors realise the importance of the green heart of the island. The mangroves may buffer Grand Cayman from hurricanes by absorbing some of the energy of storm surges, but also purify the water that runs off from the island. As essential nurseries for reef fish they are home to hundreds of species, and also act as vital refuges for land crabs. They are the only part of the island without roads between the coast and the interior, allowing land crabs to migrate to and from the water without being run over.

Mangroves in the botanical park (Photo: Stewart McPherson).

Native scrub vegetation (Photo: Stewart McPherson).

Forest in the Mastic Reserve (Photo: Stewart McPherson).

An adult blue iguana (Photo: Stewart McPherson).

Iguana eggs (Photo: Stewart McPherson).

Iguana enclosures (Photo: Stewart McPherson).

A captive iguana (Photo: Stewart McPherson).

An ivory-crested iguana (Photo: Stewart McPherson).

Wildlife

The Cayman Islands have an impressive array of wildlife, with more than 220 species of birds (of which 17 are endemic), 15 native reptiles (9 endemic), 415 native plants (30 endemic) and thousands of native invertebrates recorded thus far, dozens of which are endemic. Unlike many other Caribbean Islands, the three islands have not been connected to neighbouring islands during recent times, accounting for the high degree of endemism. The largest land animal to evolved on Grand Cayman is one of the most extraordinary. The endemic blue iguana (*Cyclura lewisi*) has a total nose-to-tail length of up to 1.5 m and a body weight of up to 14 kg. Unlike the widespread green iguana (*Iguana iguana*), Grand Cayman's endemic iguana is unique for its striking colour. In the morning, adults are typically dark grey, matching the limestone rock of their habitat. As the day warms, however, the iguanas change colour to bright, turquoise blue. The blue colouration is particularly pronounced in males and reaches its peak in the presence of other iguanas to signal and to establish territory.

The blue iguana is one of the most unusual reptiles alive today, with an equally remarkable story. Sub-fossils indicate that the species was abundant on Grand Cayman prior to the arrival of Europeans. From the 17th century onwards, European settlers hunted the animal intensively as food. Coupled with habitat loss, road kill and the introduction of predators like cats and dogs, the number of iguanas crashed. By 2003, fewer than 15 blue iguanas existed in the wild and the species was predicted to become extinct by 2010. Local conservations refused to accept this death sentence. As the blue iguana population teetered on the brink of collapse, a state that some argued was already 'functional extinction' in the wild, an ambitious project was launched by a group of conservationists from the National Trust for the Cayman Islands, led by Fred Burton. The plan was simple. In order to stop the total extinction of the species, the last wild iguanas would be captured and bred through an *ex situ* conservation programme. In 1990, Fred and his team set up the Blue Iguana Recovery Programme, bringing in six wild blue iguanas and many more caged pets that were voluntarily donated. By 1992, he had 20 founder individuals and, despite receiving no Government funding, he set up a breeding facility. Since then, over 800 blue iguanas have been hatched in captivity and then released into the wild. The local government also allocated 80 hectares of shrubland to iguana conservation to buoy these successes.

Cayman Brac and Little Cayman are also home to an endemic iguana, the Sister Isles iguana (*Cyclura nubila caymanensis*). Just 100 individuals of this yellow-brown iguana remain on Cayman Brac and a further 1500 on Little Cayman, but unlike the blue iguana they have yet to be rescued from the brink.

Fiddler crabs in the mangrove forest (Photo: Stewart McPherson).

Of the other large endemic animals, birds are by far the most numerous. The 17 endemic birds found on the islands are subspecies of a range of different bird types and include the Grand Cayman parrot (*Amazona leucocephala caymanensis*), Cayman Brac parrot (*Amazona leucocephala hesterna*), Bananaquit (*Coereba flaveola sharpei*), Northern flicker (*Colaptes auratus gundlachi*), Grand Cayman vitelline warbler (*Setophaga vitellina vitellina*), Sister Islands vitelline warbler (*Setophaga vitellina crawfordi*), Caribbean elaenia (*Elaenia martinica caymanensis*), Caribbean dove (*Leptotila jamaicensis collaris*), West Indian woodpecker (*Melanerpes superciliaris caymanensis*), Grand Cayman bullfinch (*Melopyrrha nigra*), Grand Cayman Greater Antillean grackle (*Quiscalus niger caymanensis*), Sister islands Greater Antillean grackle (*Quiscalus niger bangsi*), Western spindalis (*Spindalis zena salvini*), Red-legged thrush (*Turdus plumbeus coryi*), Loggerhead kingbird (*Tyrannus caudifasciatus caymanensis*), Thick-billed vireo (*Vireo crassirostris alleni*) and the Yucatan vireo (*Vireo magister caymanensis*).

Crabs are particularly conspicuous, and hermit crabs occur in great numbers within the islands' forests, while fiddler crabs (*Uca speciosa*) can be found in the mangroves and on muddy beaches. These crabs are immediately recognisable by their single enlarged claw, used to signal between individuals, including in mating displays and challenges to other crabs.

A hermit crab (Photo: Alexey Stiop/Shutterstock.com).

Royal terns on Grand Cayman (Photo: theHotCorner/Shutterstock.com).

The endemic race of the northern flicker (*Colaptes auratus gundlachi*) (Photo: Mike Pienkowski).

A colourful cayman parrot (Photo: Kristen Murray/Shutterstock.com).

A Cayman-endemic species; Taylor's bullfinch (*Melopyrrha taylori*) (Photo: Mike Pienkowski).

A heron fishing close to the shore (Photo: Michelle Horne/Shutterstock.com).

Tillandsia air plants in their native habitat (Photo: Stewart McPherson).

Flora

The Cayman islands were historically covered in a mosaic of different forest types, including dry forest, mangrove, wetlands and scrub. Today this coverage is more fragmented owing to human development, however examples of all vegetation types persist. About 415 species are native to the islands, and of these 21 species are endemic, with a further 8 endemic varieties of species otherwise found elsewhere. The greatest number of endemic species is found on Grand Cayman, which has the wettest and most extensive forest areas. A full 46% of native plant species are considered endangered, mainly as a result of habitat loss but also because of competition by introduced species.

The plants that have evolved on the islands have had to adapt to a climate that includes a warm wet season as well as a cool dry season, particularly because the thin soils have a relatively low capacity to retain water. Many of the trees have extremely developed roots that snake over the rocky substrate in order to establish a firm foothold, also penetrating deeply towards the water table below. Specialist Bromeliads like *Tillandsia*—best known as airplants—are capable of drawing moisture from the air itself, allowing them to survive in very dry habitats. Other plants, like the wild banana orchid (*Myrmecophila thomsoniana*), the national flower, simply drop their leaves to survive particularly dry spells, regrowing when rains return.

The extensive roots of a fig tree (Photo: Stewart McPherson).

Grand Cayman's endemic variety of the wild banana orchid (*Myrmecophilia thomsoniana* var. *thomsoniana*) growing in a clearing in the island's extensive mangrove forests (Photo: Stewart McPherson).

Marine Environment

The absence of agricultural run-off or river systems has left the Cayman islands with some of the clearest waters in the Caribbean. Grand Cayman is also home to one of the largest remaining patches of mangrove forest in the entire Caribbean. It is an important refuge for marine species and essential both as a major fish nursery and in the production of seeds of mangrove species. An extensive system of 40 marine parks are now in place to preserve the stunning underwater world of the islands, renowned amongst divers for its 360 species of native fish and 37 species of coral, as well as incredible opportunities to swim with groupers, rays and sharks.

The Cayman Islands are one of the last places in the Caribbean where large Nassau grouper (*Epinephelus striatus*) mating aggregations still take place. These fish are some of the largest found on the coral reefs of the Caymans, growing over a metre in length and weighing over 25 kg. Annual aggregation events commonly comprise 3500 individuals and see millions of eggs released. Such aggregations used to be more common across the Caribbean, but these inquisitive and easily caught fish were targeted unsustainably by fishermen across the region causing numbers to crash. As one of the last great aggregation sites, its preservation is vital, yet long term protection has not yet been established.

A mature Nassau grouper (Photo: NicolasVoisin44/Shutterstock.com).

A large haul of grouper (Photo: Grouper Moon Program).

A grouper aggregation event (Photo: Grouper Moon Program).

White sands and turquoise waters are typical of the British Virgin Islands (Photo: BlueOrange Studio/Shutterstock.com).

Population: 31 758 (2018)
Area: 153 sq. km of dry land
Currency: United States dollar
Capital: Road Town (Tortola island)
Flag: A Blue Ensign bearing the islands' coat of arms—Saint Ursula, the twelve lamps of her virgin followers and the Latin motto *vigilate* (be watchful).

BRITISH VIRGIN ISLANDS

The British Virgin Islands are an archipelago of four main islands and 56 smaller islets and cays located approximately 60 km east of Puerto Rico. About 15 of the islands are inhabited, but the vast majority of people reside on the largest island, Tortola (55 sq. km, 23 500 people), and the three other main islands, Virgin Gorda (21 sq. km, 2930 people), Jost van Dyke (9 sq. km, 298 people) and Anegada (38 sq. km, 285 people). The remaining islands are much smaller and some are privately owned and seasonally occupied. All of the British Virgin Islands are of volcanic origin except for Anegada, which is a low-lying coral island separated from the rest of the Territory's island cluster by about 30 kilometres.

The Territory's official and legal name is the Virgin Islands. However, the term British Virgin Islands is frequently used to distinguish the territory from the neighbouring United States Virgin Islands (an American territory within sight of the British Virgin Islands' westernmost point) and the confusingly named Spanish Virgin Islands (which form part of Puerto Rico, itself a territory of the United States). The term Virgin Islands Archipelago is often used to refer to all three island groups together.

The first European sighting of the Virgin Islands was made by Christopher Columbus in 1493 when, on his second voyage to the Americas, he made landfall on the islands. He gave them the fanciful name *Santa Ursula y las Once Mil Vírgenes* (Saint Ursula and her 11 000 Virgins). Although the Spanish Empire claimed the islands, they were never settled, and as their colonial power waned, the archipelago increasingly sheltered Dutch, French and English pirates who raided ships laden with gold and stashed their booty on the islands. Many of the world's most notorious pirates are known to have frequented the British Virgin Islands' waters, including Blackbeard (Edward Teach) and the feared Captain William Kidd! The first settlement was established on Tortola by the Dutch around 1648, but the island was captured by the British in 1672, annexing Anegada and Virgin Gorda eight years later.

While people appeared on the Caribbean islands about 6000 years ago, emigrating from Guiana and Venezuela as well as from Central America, little evidence of their presence has been found on the Virgin Islands. However, an indigenous American population of up to 20 000 people lived across the British Virgin Islands and are known to have cultivated cassava, spun cotton, fired pottery and carved ceremonial shell objects. Tortola has been found to harbour 33 sites that were used by prehistoric people either as permanent settlements or temporary camp sites, starting with fisher-forager communities from around BCE 600–1500! The indigenous people were initially left to live peacefully alongside the early European settlers for a matter of years, but from 1550 they were systematically exterminated, captured as slaves and shipped elsewhere or killed by infectious diseases.

British Virgin Islands

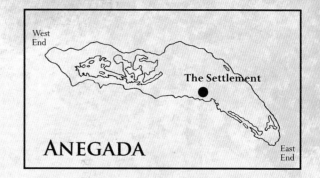

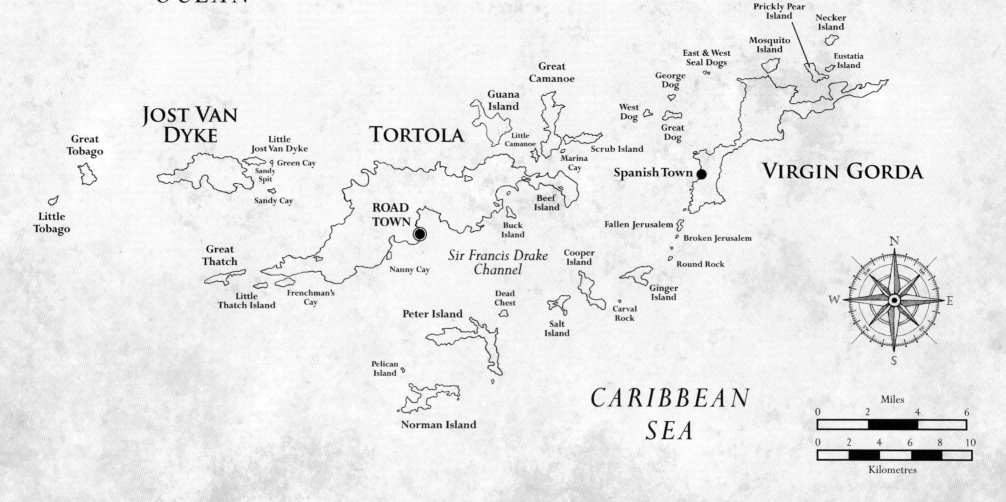

Road town, Tortola (Photo: BlueOrange Studio/Shutterstock.com).

Road Town

Road Town is the capital of the islands, sitting on a natural harbour on the island of Tortola. The name of the settlement of about 12 600 people is derived from the nautical term 'roadstead', a body of water sheltered from significant ocean swell, rip currents and spring tides that allows for ships to anchor with relative safety. It is the site of the only major airport.

Landscape and Habitats

Most of the British Virgin Islands are comprised of rugged, hilly terrain that was originally covered by Caribbean dry forest, scrub and cactus thickets, although the more elevated slopes of Tortola harbour lush moist forests comprised of hardwoods and tree ferns. Anegada is the exception; the island is entirely flat on account of its coralline form. The peak of Sage Mountain, located on Tortola's main mountain ridge, is the territory's highest point at 523 m. Tortola was formerly mined for copper, ruins of which remain today.

The sheltered south- and west-facing bays of the islands were fringed with mangrove forests, much now lost to human activities on the inhabited islands. Moving offshore, the islands' clear tropical waters support coral reefs and extensive sea-grass beds.

Mining ruins on Tortola (Photo: Simon Vacher).

Virgin Gorda (Photo: Sean Pavone/Shutterstock.com).

A male magnificent frigatebird (Photo: Andy McGowan).

A view of Great Tobago. Note the frigatebirds (Stewart McPherson).

Wildlife

A number of animal species are endemic to the British Virgin Islands, including the critically endangered Anegada Ground iguana (*Cyclura pinguis*), the Carrot Rock anole (*Anolis ernestwilliamsi*), Carrot Rock skink (*Spondylurus macleani*), the Anegada skink (*Spondylurus anegadae*), two species of blind snake (*Typhlops naugus* and *T. catapontus*), a frog—the Virgin Islands coqui (*Eleutherodactylus schwartzi*)—and dozen invertebrates, including a longhorn beetle (*Styloleptoides inflaticollis*), several butterflies and a moth, three species of spider and at least three types of shrimp!

Wildlife across the British Virgin Islands faces pressures from human settlements in the territory and beyond. This is particularly true of the islands in the west of the group, which lie close to the densely populated US Virgin Islands and Puerto Rico.

Great Tobago Island, situated in the extreme west of the British Virgin Islands, is designated as the Great Tobago National Park along with neighbouring Little Tobago. Although Great Tobago itself is just 1 sq. km in size, the island supports the third largest population of nesting magnificent frigatebirds in the entire Caribbean. It is thus one of the most important national parks in the territory.

Sadly, numbers of the frigatebirds are being decimated. Adult frigatebirds fly far out to sea into international waters to find food for their chicks. With their enormous wings and slight bodies, the birds cannot take off if immersed in water and, unlike many seabirds, do not dive into the sea to find fish. Instead, they harass other birds returning with full crops of fish, chasing them to force their victims to regurgitate in flight. As well as pirating other birds, the frigates follow fishing vessels and snatch fish as the fishermen reel in their lines. Unfortunately, the frigatebirds often ingest fish that are still attached to fishing hooks. The hooks become attached within the birds' throats and they become trapped. The fishermen have little sympathy for these 'thieves' and simply cut the fishing line to release the birds rather than remove the hooks. The birds return to their nesting sites invariably trailing tens of metres of fishing line and, as they land on their nesting trees, become quickly entangled amongst the vegetation. Parts of Great Tobago are now covered with deadly webs of nylon that kill not just the birds hooked to them, but others that fly into the tangle of fishing line as well. Frigatebirds caught on the fishing lines suffer slow and drawn out deaths. As they struggle, the lines cut deeply into their flesh; they hang in the lines starving and dehydrating in the tropical sun, the fortunate ones being those quickly suffocated by the tangle of line that do not have to endure days of exposure. Such an end is unfitting for any creature.

Nesting frigatebirds (Photo: Stewart McPherson).

Fishing line attached to a frigatebird's corpse (Photo: Stewart McPherson).

A mature specimen of the Anegada ground iguana (*Cyclura pinguis*) (Photo: Kelly Bradley, Fort Worth Zoo).

The imperilled Anegada Rock Iguana is a large, muscular lizard almost 1 metre in length. Formerly widespread, they were historically hunted for food, being both large and tasty, and are now restricted to Anegada and small, restored populations on Guana, Mosquito, Necker and Norman islands. While no longer hunted, feral cats, dogs and rats prey upon juvenile iguanas and continue to devastate the remaining rock iguanas on Anegada.

In 1997 the British Virgin Islands National Parks Trust set up the Anegada Rock Iguana Headstart Facility in an ambitious project to save the species from extinction. The logic adopted in this conservation effort differed from that used in the Blue Iguana Recovery Programme on the Cayman Islands: rather than breed iguanas in captivity and introduce their offspring into the wild, the Headstart Facility centres on giving juvenile rock iguanas a better chance of surviving in the wild to increase rates of natural breeding.

Currently about 30–40 juvenile iguanas are caught annually and allowed to grow in safety before being released after a couple of years when they are larger and able to fend better for themselves. As a result, the survival rate of the released iguanas is now 79% in the wild, greatly reducing the juvenile mortality rate. As of November 2015, 206 iguanas have been given a head start and returned to the wild, and the wild population of approximately 200 lizards has burgeoned to between 400 and 500 animals!

Juvenile Anegada iguana at the British Virgin Islands National Parks Trust's Anegada Rock Iguana Headstart Facility on Anegada (Photo: Samantha Addinall).

American flamingos (*Phoenicopterus ruber*) in Anegada's salt ponds - the entire population was wiped out, but then reintroduced by the British Virgin Islands National Parks Trust. Large flocks can now be seen once again (Photo: Mike Pienkowski).

A green heron (*Butorides virescens*) perched on mangrove roots (Photo: Mike Pienkowski).

Flora

The British Virgin Islands are home to many native species, including a few endemics, like the Anegada Poke-me-boy (*Acacia anegadensis*), the Wire Wist (*Metastelma anegadense*), a bromeliad known only from Guana Island (*Pitcairnia jareckii*) and Kiaerskov's Lidflower (*Calyptranthes kiaerskovii*), formerly known also from Puerto Rico, but now known only on Virgin Gorda and Tortola.

The introduction of pest animals like feral goats has had a tremendous impact on the islands' flora. The goats consume virtually all types of plant, with the exception of the spiniest cacti. As a result, in some places, the ground is thick with spiny *Opuntia repens*, or the ground left bare, damaged and prone to erosion. However, attempts to eradicate goats on some of the islands have been successful, and native vegetation has proliferated.

Regeneration of native forest offers significant benefits. The islands are home to four species of mangrove trees, the white (*Laguncularia racemosa*), red (*Rhizophora mangle*), black (*Avicennia germinans*) and buttonwood (*Conocarpus erectus*) mangroves. Mangrove forests, previously cleared out of ignorance, are now recognised as vital barriers against storm surges. As the islands recover in the aftermath of September 2017 hurricanes Irma and Maria, the importance of natural defences to the islands cannot be overstated.

The beautiful orchid (*Psychillis macconnelliae*) occurs only across Puerto Rico and the Virgin Islands Archipelago (Photo: Nancy Woodfield Pascoe).

Cactus growing on Great Tobago (Photo: Stewart McPherson).

Marine Environment

The British Virgin Islands have 380 sq. km of coral reefs that range in size from small fragments of a few square metres to the Anegada Horseshoe reef which is made up of close to 77 sq. km of coral. This magnificent living structure is 29 kilometres long and the largest barrier coral reef in the Caribbean and the fourth largest on Earth. Reef life includes approximately 400 species of fish, including colourful damsel fish, angel fish, box fish, butterfly fish, puffers, grunts, seahorses and eels, while other animals like lobsters, nudibranchs (sea slugs) and tube worms are common. Larger predators include barracuda, snapper and jacks, while nurse and tiger sharks are occasionally spotted. The scuba diving industry is well established across the islands, with snorkellers well catered for also.

The waters around the island are certainly breathtaking to behold and reputed to be some of the most brilliantly coloured in the region. An unusual geological formation known as "The Baths" located on the southern end of the island of Virgin Gorda is one of the Virgin Islands' major tourist destinations. At The Baths, in spite of the island's largely volcanic origins, huge granite boulders lie in piles on the beach, forming scenic, picture-perfect grottoes that are open to the sea, reminiscent of the coast of Mahé (the Seychelles) in the Indian Ocean.

A beautiful tube worm (Photo: Kyle Lippenberger/Shutterstock.com).

Schooling blue tangs and surgeonfish (Photo: BCampbell65/Shutterstock.com).

A school of silversides (Photo: BCampbell65/Shutterstock.com)

When explorer Robert Schomburgk, carried out the first survey of Anegada in 1831, the detailed report and map that he sent to the Royal Geographical Society in London made mention of "Heaps of Conch Shells" at the island's eastern tip. To this day, visitors to the eastern end of Anegada cannot miss the gigantic mounds of tens of thousands of large shells that dominate the islands vast salt ponds.

All of the shells belong to the queen conch (*Lobatus gigas*), one of the world's largest and most beautiful gastropods, each with a shell up to 35 cm long. Some of the smaller shell heaps inland have been lying exposed to the elements for centuries such that they have turned grey, like limestone. These are thought to be the discarded shells of conchs consumed by indigenous islanders.

The largest heaps, of more recent origin, are contrastingly bright and colourful; these are separated from the shoreline by mangrove forests up to 100 metres across, and individual heaps may be 30 metres in diameter and 4 metres high! It is thought that the shells are discarded in this way in specific locations to avoid wasting time when fishing for live conchs, the empty shells being frustrating decoys. Queen conchs have long been a valued and extremely sought after food item, sadly, populations have crashed across the Caribbean owing to rampant overfishing, as these vast middens attest to.

An adult queen conch raised in captivity (Photo: Stewart McPherson).

Middens formed from discarded conch shells (Photo: Stewart McPherson).

Detail of conch shells in an offshore midden (Photo: Stewart McPherson).

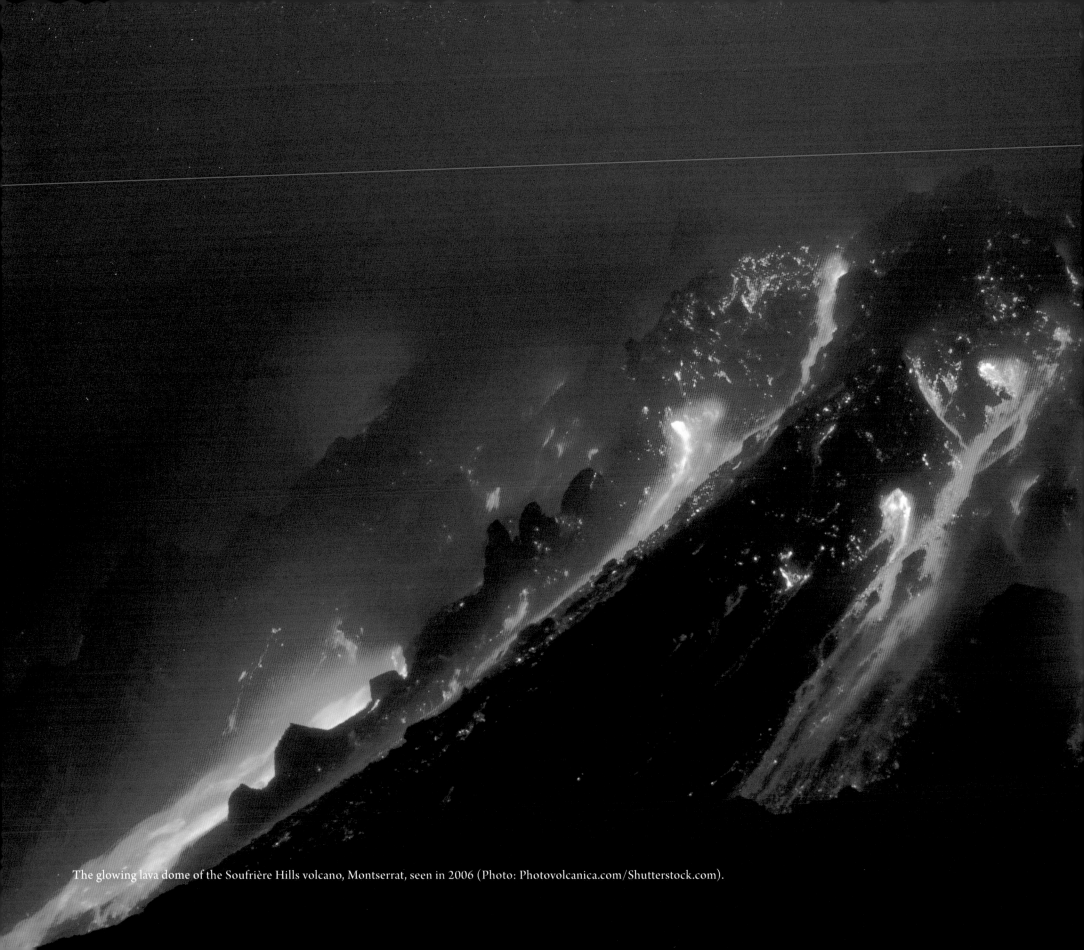

The glowing lava dome of the Soufrière Hills volcano, Montserrat, seen in 2006 (Photo: Photovolcanica.com/Shutterstock.com).

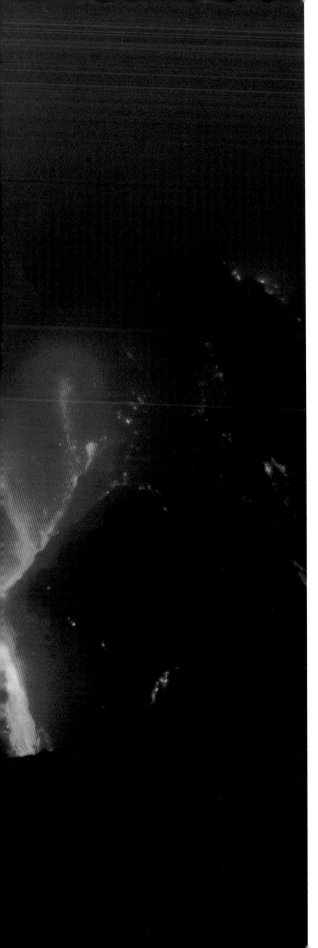

Population: 5200 (2018)
Area: 102 sq. km of dry land
Currency: East Caribbean Dollar
Capital: Brades (*de facto*)
Flag: A Blue Ensign bearing the Montserrat coat of arms—the female figure of Erin and the harp are symbols of Ireland.

MONTSERRAT

Montserrat is one of the Leeward Islands in the Lesser Antilles chain in the eastern Caribbean. It is situated 43 km southwest of Antigua and 64 km northwest of Guadeloupe. The island, which is shaped like a tear-drop and about 17 km long and 11 wide, is volcanic in origin and currently experiencing a period of volcanic activity. Following centuries of dormancy, in July 1995 the island's Soufrière Hills volcano began to erupt in a prolonged 1995–1999 eruption event. The capital, Plymouth, was evacuated soon after the eruption began as dangerous pyroclastic flows (currents of superheated gas and volcanic debris that may travel at up to 700 km/hour with a temperature of 1000 ºC!) began to occur, spreading vast quantities of ash across the southern part of the island. In late August of the same year an explosive eruption occurred, followed by two more major explosive events during the next two years, along with numerous pyroclastic flows. This explosive activity blanketed Plymouth under 5–12 metres of ash and mud. The entire southern half of the island was designated an exclusion zone from which all visitors are excluded to this day without special permit. The 25 June 1997 eruption generated a pyroclastic flow that tragically killed 19 civilians who had remained within the exclusion zone, and destroyed the airport and harbour.

The eruptive phase continues, but with more sporadic eruption events taking place in December 2006, July 2008 and February 2010. Thus far, 17 settlements have been destroyed and another dozen abandoned. Two thirds of the island's 1995 population (about 7000 people) left Montserrat, over half of which emigrated to the UK. These refugees were granted leave to remain in the UK in 1998, and were given British citizenship in 2002. Nonetheless, a proportion still campaign for their return to the island now that conditions and infrastructure have improved in the north of the island, where the new centre of government was established at Brades in 1998.

Known as "the Emerald Isle of the Caribbean", Montserrat's rugged slopes are clad with lush, tropical rainforest and exquisite streams and waterfalls. The island was first sighted by Christopher Columbus in 1493, who named it Santa María de Montserrat, after the Benedictine Santa Maria de Montserrat monastery on Montserrat Mountain near Barcelona, Spain. The island was previously inhabited by indigenous American Arawaks who were driven from the island around the mid 1400s by the aggressive Carib people. Spain did not colonise Montserrat, but by the start of the 17th century, a ragged European community existed on the island, though little is known of who these settlers were. Settlement finally began in 1632, when Sir Thomas Warner, the first British Governor of Saint Kitts, organised a group of English settlers and Redlegs (Irish Catholic prisoners of war sold into slavery) to migrate to the island. Montserrat was thus officially settled for the first time and under British rule.

Montserrat

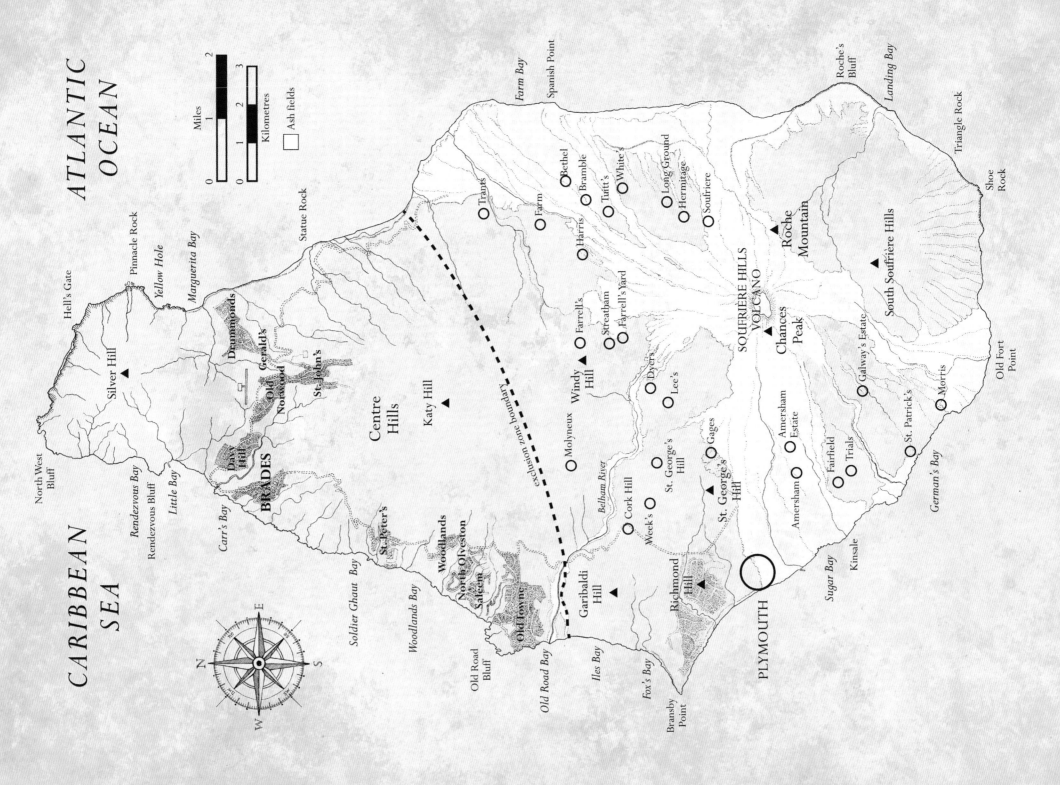

When Montserrat was settled, the Irish slaves greatly outnumbered the English, making up 69% of the island's European population in 1637. More Irish immigrants subsequently arrived from Virginia and many plantations were set up to cultivate tobacco, indigo and, later, cotton and sugar, being the primary industries of the region.

By the late 17th century, many of the initial Irish settlers previously indentured as labourers were free, and some became plantation managers and owners. St Patrick's Day is still celebrated as a public holiday and the symbol of the shamrock plant is seen widely across the island. The Irish Harp graces Montserrat's flag along with Erin, the female personification of Ireland, and to this day Irish surnames remain widespread.

During the 18th century, thousands of Africans were kidnapped from their homelands and sold into slavery to work on the plantations of Montserrat under the threat of the whip and the gallows. The colonists built a slave-driven economy based on the production of sugar, rum, arrowroot and sea island cotton. When slavery ended on the island in 1834, those of African descent represented the majority of the population, numbering approximately 7000 in total. Today's Montserratians are a mix of a number of ethnic groups, including black, white and creole, but the population is predominantly of mixed African-Irish descent.

Montserrat, as illustrated in 1860 (Photo: Marzolino/Shutterstock.com)

Ruins of a sugar mill dating from 1773 (Photo: Stewart McPherson)

The devastated remains of Plymouth, a grey landscape in an island otherwise famous for its lush greenery (Photo: Stewart McPherson).

Plymouth

Plymouth remains the *de jure* capital of Montserrat and is thus the world's only ghost-town capital with a population of zero! The city had a population of about 4000 people in 1995, when the Soufrière Hills volcano began erupting, and was permanently evacuated following the 25 June 1997 eruption. While government currently sits at Brades, a town of 1000 inhabitants on the northwest coast that has been *de facto* capital since 1998, a new capital is being constructed at nearby Little Bay.

Today, the Plymouth settlement sits empty in the southwest corner of the exclusion zone, in some places covered in ash several storeys high such that only the tops of buildings, the roofs of houses or chimneys show, whilst in other places the rubble strewn streets are more or less clear. Given the sudden departure of the population, the buildings that survived the blistering heat of the pyroclastic flows remain more or less as they were left, their contents sometimes intact, but more usually covered in ash that tore through splintering windows as the eruption enveloped the landscape.

Whilst still off limits, roads to the exclusion zone have been cleared and there are now tourist platforms in place that offer a glimpse of the volcano itself. Ruined Plymouth, remains strictly out of bounds for the time being, but may itself become a point of interest for the island's increasing tourism.

A ruined building in Plymouth (Photo: Gorb Andrii/Shutterstock.com).

Clearance works are ongoing (Photo: Stewart McPherson).

Landscape and Habitats

Montserrat is a volcanic island formed atop a submarine bank criss-crossed by fault zones. The north of the island was formed first, during eruptions that started about 2.6 million years ago, the central region about 950 000 years ago and the southern part a geologically young 130 000 years ago. The Soufrière Hills volcano sits in the centre of the southern region and, prior to its 1995 eruption, was 1000 metres tall at its highest point, Chance's Peak. To date, the volcano remains restive, with periodic tremors and releases of gas and sometimes ash, however there have been no eruptions or pyroclastic flows since 2005.

Naturally, a fair proportion of the southern half of the island is covered in various types of lava, and ash lies thick in many areas, particularly valley floors. However, the overwhelming majority of Montserrat is lush with greenery. The island has a tropical climate with temperatures virtually always in the 23–30 ºC range, with ample rainfall throughout the year, but particularly from August to November. Given the deep, rich volcanic soil, forest growth is luxuriant.

The island also supports a number of coral reefs, both around the main island as well as the two offshore islets Virgin and Statue Rock, while coastal caves are important habitats for some of the eight native bat species.

The volcano's lava dome (Photo: Photovolcanica.com/Shutterstock.com).

Vegetation recovering around Plymouth (Photo: Gorb Andrii/Shutterstock.com).

An active volcanic vent (Photo: Adrian Reynolds/Shutterstock.com).

Feral donkeys wander the ruins of Plymouth (Photo: Stewart McPherson).

Wildlife

Despite its small size, Montserrat supports an impressive range of wildlife, including 76 species of birds, 9 native reptiles and 9 mammals (8 species of bats and the agouti). The diversity of invertebrates is less well known, but the island's lush rainforests are rich in arthropod life, particularly beetles. A partial inventory in 2005 found 718 invertebrate species in 63 families, with at least 81 species that may be endemic.

Endemic birds include the national bird, the Montserrat oriole (*Icterus oberi*) and a Montserrat-endemic subspecies of the forest thrush (*Turdus lherminieri dorotheae*). There is also an endemic subspecies of the yellow-shouldered bat (*Sturnira thomasi vulcanensis*), while endemic reptiles include the galliwasp lizard (*Diploglossus montisserrati*), an anole (*Anolis lividus*), the Montserrat skink (*Mabuya montserratae*), the Montserrat ameiva (*Ameiva pluvianotata*—also a lizard), the Montserrat blindsnake (*Typhlops monastus*) and the Montserrat racer (*Alsophis manselli*).

More than 10% of Montserrat's native invertebrates are endemic, including two species of net-winged beetle, a longhorn beetle (*Strangalia benitoespinali*), a darkling beetle (*Nesocyrtosoma lacrima*), an undescribed bombardier beetle, a forest cricket, a new species of wasp and the beautiful Montserrat tarantula (*Cyrtopholis femoralis*).

Remains of a land crab on the arid devastation plain (Photo: Stewart McPherson).

A native bat (Photo: Stewart McPherson).

A Montserrat anole at rest (Photo: Nicolas Tirard/Shutterstock.com).

The Montserrat galliwasp (*Diploglossus montisserrati*) (Photo: Carole McCauley).

An adult male Montserrat oreole (*Icterus oberi*). This species is unique to Montserrat's forest (Photo: Mike Pienkowski).

The advent of the volcanic eruption was not only a disaster for the people living on Montserrat. A number of species on the island were already regarded as critically endangered when the eruption took place and this cataclysmic event only exacerbated their perilous positions.

Fears arose in particular for Montserrat's most secretive animal, the galliwasp lizard, thought to be restricted to a tiny fragment of forest just 1.5 hectares in size on the west side of the island. Many believed that the entire population may have been wiped out as the island was carpeted with ash. Fortunately, several sightings of the galliwasp have been made during the past decade, so the species appears to have survived and its habitat is now strictly protected.

Similarly, the habitat of the endemic oriole was totally destroyed by the volcano, yet after extensive searches, about 200 of the birds were found in hills to the north of the volcano. In 1998, eight rescued orioles were sent to the UK where they have been successfully bred by the Durrell Wildlife trust.

The blanket of ash that covered the island also greatly impacted the production of nectar bearing flowers and edible fruits by native plants; the native bats were devastated by the scarcity of their primary food sources. The fine, acidic ash even caused their fur to fall out, in addition to eroding their teeth, such was the coating of ash on what little fruit they could find.

A purple-throated carib hummingbird (Photo: Alistair Homer/Shutterstock.com).

The Montserrat endemic subspecies of forest thrush (*Cichlherminia lherminieri dorotheae*) (Photo: Mike Pienkowski).

An even more troubling fate befell one of Montserrat's most iconic native animals, one which has suffered not just from the string of natural disasters, but which has also became the victim of a disease with no effective cure to date. The mountain chicken (*Leptodactylus fallax*) is one of the largest frogs in the world and certainly the largest in the Caribbean, with the bigger females weighing up to 1 kg and stretching to over 40 cm in length from snout to rear toes. This magnificent frog was historically present on seven Caribbean islands, but has been driven extinct on all except Montserrat and Dominica.

The reason for this decline is hinted at in its common name. The frogs, whose large thighs are a delicacy of traditional Caribbean cooking, taste like delicately flavoured chicken. A a result, the animals were hunted in great numbers, up to 36 000 frogs per year in Dominica until it became protected. Habitat loss and increasingly violent hurricanes compounded their decline, but the greatest shock of all arrived in the form of an infectious disease, chytridiomycosis, caused by a deadly fungus (*Batrachochytrium dendrobatidis*) which is decimating frog populations worldwide. The fungus ravaged the mountain chickens and wiped out most known populations. A reservoir population in captivity is being used to attempt reintroductions, but conservationists face an uphill battle as the fungus persists in the wild and a means of combating its deadly symptoms needs to be established.

A healthy adult mountain chicken (*Leptodactylus fallax*). The confusing name is derived from the similarity of its flesh to chicken. Local custom saw these frogs hunted for their large, muscular hind legs, much valued in traditional dishes (Photo: Mike Pienkowski).

A frog killed by the chytrid fungus (Photo: Adams Durrell).

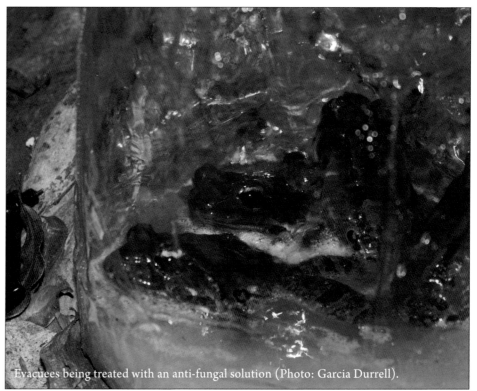

Evacuees being treated with an anti-fungal solution (Photo: Garcia Durrell).

Native vegetation in a forest reserve (Photo: Stewart McPherson).

Flora

Being a lush tropical island, there is a broad assemblage of plant species on Montserrat, amounting to over 700 species in total, including at least 132 tree species. The vegetation varies according to levels of rainfall, which of course is closely linked to elevation; drier scrub and coastal vegetation is associated with the lowlands and coastlines, while dry forests are present further inland. As elevation increases the vegetation gives way to deciduous woodland and, higher, tropical wet forest and tree fern groves. The very highest areas include windswept bonsai cloud forests, though these habitats are limited and threatened by volcanic activity.

There are three plants endemic to the island of Montserrat. The endemic orchid *Epidendrum montserratense* was feared extinct, but significant populations are now known, including on trees killed by the volcanic eruption. Similarly the pribby (Rondeletia buxifolia), a relative of coffee, was also thought to have been wiped out. Both were rediscovered in 2006 and are now maintained in botanical garden collections with reintroductions made on Montserrat. Unfortunately, the entire known habitat of the third unique plant, *Xylosma serrata*, was destroyed by the lava flows and ash falls of the late 1990s. To date, no further populations have been discovered and the species is presumed to have been rendered extinct.

The endemic orchid *Epidendrum montserratense* (Photo: Martin A. Hamilton, Royal Botanic Gardens, Kew).

Pink petals cover the forest floor (Photo: Stewart McPherson).

Marine Environment

Montserrat supports extensive coral reefs, many of which were affected by ash falls following the volcanic eruption. The fine, silty ash drifted down onto the reefs and smothered them, blocking out light and oxygen, leading to significant coral die off. Even so, in the years that followed, the reefs began to recover, not least because of the rich mineral components of the damaging ash.

However, the reefs of Montserrat, like almost all other parts of the Caribbean, are impacted by the encroachment of an alien species—the lionfish. Native to the waters of the Indo-Pacific, lionfish were first spotted in the waters off Florida in 1985, either resulting from discarded pets or the inadvertent transfer of eggs or fish fry to the ocean in the ballast waters of cargo ships. Since then, two species, *Pterois volitans* and *P. miles*, have spread rapidly across the Caribbean. With no native predators adapted to avoid their venomous spines and consume them, these voracious fish have reproduced exponentially, decimating populations of native fish. To combat their plague proportions, divers on Montserrat and islands across the Caribbean hunt the lionfish to cull their numbers, using specialised spear guns and traps to bring thousands ashore each year. Their tasty meat is now often sold to encourage their consumption and to fund culling expeditions!

A cuttlefish resting on volcanic sand (Photo: Blue-sea.cz/Shutterstock.com).

The invasive lionfish (Photo: Chris K Horne/Shutterstock.com).

Spearing lionfish to protect native reef species (Photo: Simon Vacher).

A brown booby colony on the Anguilla coast (Photo: Stewart McPherson).

Population: 14 764 (2016)
Area: 91 sq. km of dry land
Currency: Eastern Caribbean dollar
Capital: The Valley
Flag: A Blue Ensign bearing the Anguilla coat of arms—three dolphins, representing friendship, wisdom and strength.

ANGUILLA

Anguilla is situated in the Leeward Islands of the Lesser Antilles, lying approximately 130 km east of the British Virgin Islands and 8 km north of the French overseas collective of Saint Martin. The island's name is derived from the Spanish *anguila*, meaning "eel", in reference to its shape; it is 25 km long but only up to 5 km wide. It was also formerly known as Snake Island during colonial times for the same reason. Anguilla, Saint Martin and Saint Barthélemy make up the Caribbean's Renaissance Islands group.

Anguilla's main island is made of coralline limestone. It is flat and low-lying, the highest point being Crocus Hill, which rises to just 65 m. The terrain consists of rocky plains interspersed with many large, lagoon-like salt ponds that occupy sea-level depressions that occur across the island.

The first European to have conclusively sighted Anguilla was the French Huguenot explorer René Goulaine de Laudonnière, during his voyages of 1564 and 1565. From this period, Europeans were referring to the island as Anguilla, but no attempts were made to set up colonies on the island during the 16th century. Some historians argue that the island was sighted by Christopher Columbus in 1493, however while Columbus journeyed close to Anguilla while exploring the Lesser Antilles during his second voyage to the New World the route that he took through the Lesser Antilles has never been established. He documented several islands that could represent Anguilla, but none definitively, and it is quite possible that he passed by without ever seeing the island.

In 1650, the island was settled by English migrants from the neighbouring island of Saint Kitts, who landed on Anguilla and established the first permanent European settlement near Road Bay. Charles de Rochfort was one of the first to document the settlement, noting in 1658 that it had been located, "at the part [of the island] where it is widest, there is a lake around which a few English families settled for seven or eight years and where they cultivated tobacco." The first settlers to arrive apparently found tobacco growing wild on the island where it had been cultivated by the island's former inhabitants, indigenous Americans.

Archaeological artefacts suggest that the indigenous population, the Taíno people, occupied the island up till some point in the 16th century. The reason for their disappearance is unknown, but it is possible that they were taken by the Spanish as slaves during the conquest of the region or killed by diseases brought to the islands by Europeans. Although populations of indigenous people were wiped out on Anguilla, they persisted on neighbouring islands like Dominica, and conflicts are known to have taken place. In 1656, the English settlers were raided by an indigenous tribe, resulting in the death of most of the men in the colony, their children and wives being taken as slaves. As a result, by 1660, Anguilla officially received the protection of the British Crown.

Anguilla

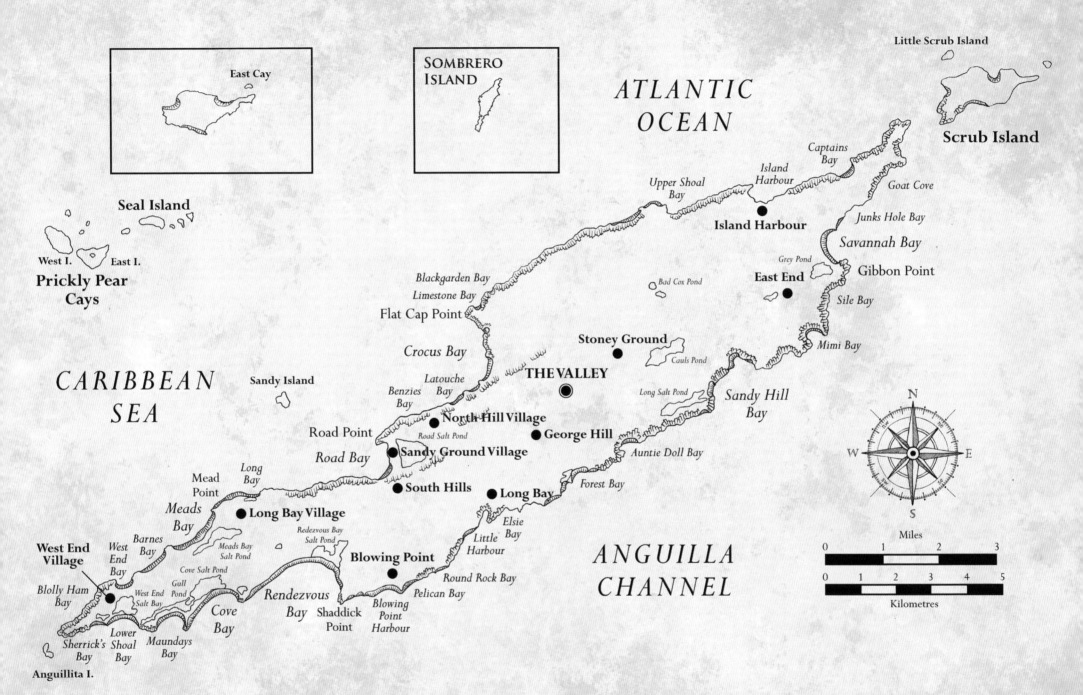

Little Scrub Island

ATLANTIC OCEAN

East Cay

SOMBRERO ISLAND

Scrub Island

Captains Bay

Island Harbour

Goat Cove

Upper Shoal Bay

Junks Hole Bay

Seal Island

Savannah Bay

Island Harbour

Grey Pond

West I. *East I.*

Prickly Pear Cays

Blackgarden Bay

Bad Cox Pond

East End

Gibbon Point

Limestone Bay

Sile Bay

Flat Cap Point

Mimi Bay

Stoney Ground

CARIBBEAN SEA

Crocus Bay

Cauls Pond

THE VALLEY

Sandy Island

Latouche Bay

Long Salt Pond

Benzies Bay

Sandy Hill Bay

North Hill Village

George Hill

Road Point

Road Salt Pond

Road Bay

Sandy Ground Village

Auntie Doll Bay

N

Mead Point

Long Bay

South Hills

Long Bay

Forest Bay

W E

Meads Bay

Long Bay Village

Redezvous Bay Salt Pond

S

Barnes Bay

West End Village

West End Bay

Meads Bay Salt Pond

Elsie Bay

ANGUILLA CHANNEL

Miles

Blolly Ham Bay

Cove Salt Pond

Little Harbour

0   1   2   3

Blowing Point

Gull Pond

Round Rock Bay

0 1 2 3 4 5

West End Salt Bay

Cove Bay

Rendezvous Bay

Pelican Bay

Kilometres

Sherrick's Bay

Lower Shoal Bay

Maundays Bay

Shaddick Point

Blowing Point Harbour

Anguillita I.

The archaeological evidence unearthed on Anguilla is some of the best preserved in the Caribbean. The ancestors of the Taíno brought sophisticated shamanic religions from South America, and discoveries in Anguilla's bat-filled caves suggest that the island became an important ceremonial centre, possibly attracting religious pilgrims from across the Renaissance Islands and beyond.

During the past forty years, exploration of the cave systems has revealed tens of thousands of artefacts, as well as dozens of ancient rock carvings on the cave walls. These finds also make Anguilla one of the richest archaeological sites in all of the Caribbean. Caves of note are now preserved by a National Trust team, and include Fountain Cavern, in which concentric circles representing the eyes of spirits are etched into the rock, along with faces in ceremonial head-dress, emblems representing their Rainbow God, Cap Juluca, and a statue carved from a stalagmite depicting the supreme deity of the Taíno. Another site of note is Big Springs, a cavernous limestone overhang sheltering a sink hole and small pools of brackish water fed by a spring. On the rough, rock walls under the overhang, dozens of faint pairs of eyes and faces glare outwards from the walls, and more than sixty carvings are known from the site! The great number of carvings and artefacts indicate that these two sites were probably of great religious significance to the Taíno.

Taíno cave-wall engravings (Photo: Stewart McPherson).

Cave art with ancient religious significance (Photo: Stewart McPherson).

Bats congregate on a cave ceiling (Photo: Stewart McPherson).

Landing in Anguilla (Photo: Stewart McPherson).

The Valley

The Valley is the capital of Anguilla and is located on the north coast of the middle of the island. It is one of twelve settlements scattered evenly across the island, each with up to several hundred inhabitants. The inhabitants are predominantly English speaking, although a number of people speak a creole derived from English and a number of African languages. These languages became established on the island as a result of the forced relocation and enslavement of Africans from several different countries during the time of the slave trade.

Since the island was administered from St Kitts from 1825—and before then from Antigua—there are few examples of colonial architecture. In fact, the island was administered as part of St Kitts and Nevis when those territories were granted internal autonomy. It was only in 1980 that the territory was able to secede from Saint Kitts and Nevis to become a separate Crown colony and eventually a UK Overseas Territory.

One of the oldest buildings is Wallblake House, a heritage plantation building constructed in 1787 by a sugar planter, Will Blake. The structure, which functions as a museum and also as the rectory of an adjacent church, includes a stables, preserved kitchens and also slave quarters. Remains of the settlement's Old Court House sit atop Crocus Hill, the island's highest point.

Sandy Ground beach on the Anguilla mainland (Photo: Kristopher Kettner/Shutterstock.com).

Landscape and Habitats

Like many coral islands, Anguilla is flat, rocky and covered with very poor soils. The varied coastline comprises fractured cliffs, coves and extensive sandy beaches. Due to the porosity of the island's fabric, there are no rivers on Anguilla and few naturally occurring sources of fresh water.

The island first formed 20 to 30 million years ago as a submarine reef atop fragments of continent that sat on the slowly sinking Caribbean tectonic plate. As the fragments of immersed land subsided beneath the waves, coral continued to grow on top of them towards the light, forming a cap of coral up to 60 metres deep. In more recent geological history, the South American plate was pushed under the Caribbean plate and began to lift it up. Possibly as recently as 2 million years ago, the reef that gave rise to modern Anguilla was lifted up out of the sea and began to be colonised by plants and animals.

The dry forests that once colonised the island were all but destroyed during the 19th century when they were burned to produce charcoal. Today, a low scrub dominates the island, consisting of tall, scratchy bushes and cacti, as well as a number of native flowering species. In addition to having a seasonally dry climate with low levels of rainfall, most of Anguilla has virtually no topsoil, and so many of the plants grow on bare, fissured slabs of limestone, often in eroded hollows where moisture may accumulate.

Only scrub can survive on the rocky soils in most places (Photo: Stewart McPherson).

Native vegetation, including cacti (Photo: Simon Vacher).

A salt pond habitat on Anguilla (Photo: Stewart McPherson).

An Anguilla bank anole (Photo: Mark Yokoyama/Shutterstock.com).

Wildlife

Although Anguilla and its satellite islands are comparatively young, their relative isolation has allowed for a number of endemic species to evolve, in particular amongst reptiles and invertebrates.

Two lizards are restricted entirely to the offshore islands of Anguilla, namely the Censky's or Little Scrub ground lizard (*Ameiva corax*), restricted to Little Scrub, a tiny islet off Scrub island, and the Sombrero ground lizard (*Ameiva corvina*), found only on Sombrero island.

Among invertebrates, a species of sweat bee (*Lasioglossum sombrerense*) and a camel spider (*Antillotrecha iviei*) have been described from Sombrero Island, while Anguilla is home to the comb-clawed beetle (*Hymenorus anguillae*).

The local islands are also home to endangered species that are regionally endemic to the Lesser Antilles, including the Anguilla bank anole (*Anolis gingivinus*), the Leeward Island racer (*Alsophis rijgersmaei*), a snake found on the main island and Scrub island, and the Lesser Antillean iguana (*Iguana delicatissima*), a species that is threatened throughout its range. On Anguilla only about 50 animals remain, and these face competition from non-native Green iguanas that arrived on the island in 1995 on rafts of vegetation generated by a hurricane.

A Little Scrub ground lizard (Photo: Stewart McPherson).

A red-footed tortoise (Photo: Stewart McPherson).

What the islands lack in species diversity amongst mammals and reptiles is more than made up for by the great number of recorded birds.

Thus far, over 135 different species of bird have been noted on the islands, of which a third are regarded as resident species. These are especially prevalent across the island's eleven major salt ponds—the largest of which has a surface area greater than 1 sq. km—all of which are designated as Important Bird Areas by Birdlife International, as well its smaller salt ponds, of which there are about a dozen.

At first glance, most visitors to Anguilla dismiss the salt ponds as wastelands of stagnant water, but for those willing to look more closely, they are shimmering magnets for vast numbers of birds. The shallow waters of each pool teem with crustaceans that attract land birds, water birds, and even birds from North America that migrate past the islands each year on their voyage to South America. The concentration of birdlife at the ponds can be staggering!

Anguilla's many offshore cays are amongst the most spectacular in the Caribbean, being major nesting sites for at least 16 different species of seabirds that are present during the breeding season. Of these, four different cays have been identified as Important Bird Areas by Birdlife International owing to the congregations of regionally and globally significant nesting sites.

Recorded species include colourful bananaquits (*Coereba flaveola*) and yellow warblers (*Setophaga petechia*), which can often be seen flitting through the air, while elegant snowy egrets (*Egretta thula*), black-necked stilts (*Himantopus mexicanus*) and short-billed dowitchers (*Limnodromus griseus*) wade through the salty shallows in search of prey. Countless other species frequent the ponds in search of food, also plucking spiders and insects from the vegetation nearby. Several of Anguilla's salt ponds are privately owned and unprotected, so they could be destroyed for development in the future.

Savannah Bay, Anguilla (Photo: Thierry Dehove/Shutterstock.com).

Two short-billed dowitchers (*Limnodromus griseus*) (Photo: Mike Pienkowski).

An Antillean bullfinch (Photo: Napa/Shutterstock.com).

Snowy egret (*Egretta thula*) (Photo: Mike Pienkowski).

A pair of black-necked stilts (*Himantopus mexicanus*) (Photos: Mike Pienkowski).

Magnificent frigatebirds on Dog Island (Photo: Stewart McPherson).

A brown noddy (*Anous stolidus*), one of hundreds that nest on Little Scrub Island (Photo: Stewart McPherson).

A brown booby (Photo: Simon Vacher).

A brown booby (Photo: Simon Vacher).

Dog Island

One of the most celebrated bird colonies of Anguilla is on Dog Island, a strip of land 2.8 km long and 1.5 km wide situated 15 km northwest of the Anguilla mainland. The middle of the island is dominated by tall thickets of scrub and prickly pear, but the coasts are dominated by rocky shoreline where birds of many species congregate. Brown boobies (*Sula leucogaster*) are common along the island's paths, while in some areas hundreds of frigatebirds (*Fregata magnificens*) nest directly on the ground in a habitat very different to that occupied by this species in the British Virgin Islands. Across the entire island, the total number of seabirds almost defies belief. While the frigatebird colony totals at about 310 pairs, it pales into insignificance next to the 113 000 pairs of sooty terns that nest nearby—one of the largest colonies for that species in the entire Caribbean region. Dog Island's list of birds continues with 600 pairs of aforementioned brown boobies, 365 pairs of laughing gulls, 190 pairs of brown noddies, 46 pairs of bridled terns, 42 pairs of masked boobies, 15 pairs of red-billed tropicbirds, 5 pairs of American oyster catchers and 3 pairs of least terns.

The quarter of a million seabirds that nest here form an essential part of the ecosystem for hundreds of kilometres in all directions. Once upon a time the island was invaded by rats, but the National Trust undertook an ambitious and successful project to eradicate them using rodent poison; the island was declared rat-free in 2014. Sadly, the island is privately owned and currently listed for sale, thus its future as an important reserve remains uncertain.

The large red throat pouches of male frigatebirds stand out even from some distance (Photo: Janielle Richardson).

Flora

Only a single species of flowering plant is endemic to Anguilla, namely the Anguilla Bush (*Rondeletia anguillensis*), with its formidably defended rosettes of tiny leaves scattered amongst rigid, woody spines that deter foraging herbivores. It grows alongside the native hollow wood (*Comocladia dodonaea*), whose leaves deliver a powerful sting that can blister human skin!

The scrub that now dominates wild parts of the island consists of tall, scratchy bushes and cacti, but does also contain many beautiful native flowering species, such as wild frangipani (*Plumeria alba*), with their soft and incredibly fragrant flowers. The branches of many bushes are festooned with the silver-blushed rosettes of the airplant *Tillandsia utriculata*. This specialised bromeliad collects rain water and dead leaves in wells between its foliage; it can grow anywhere that it can perch.

The most beautiful and unusual Anguillan plant occurs in the extreme east of the island, along the narrow 4 km long peninsula that extends towards Dog Island. This area is virtually uninhabited and is the most barren and rocky corner of the Anguillan mainland. Across the peninsula's windswept plains grow exquisite groves of Turk's head cactus (*Melocactus intortus*). Clusters of these beautiful green barrels, each with its own cap of red are set against the brilliant blue of the Caribbean water; a sight that is truly special to Anguilla!

Rondeletia anguillensis, Anguilla's sole endemic plant (Photo: Martin A. Hamilton, Royal Botanic Gardens, Kew).

The striking Turk's head cactus in eastern Anguilla (Photo: Stewart McPherson).

Marine Environment

The waters around Anguilla are largely pristine, thanks to the island's important tourism market, which ensures that its beaches remain clean and that waste is disposed of away from the ocean. Given its tropical situation, the reefs of the island are very rich, and include a broad variety of abundant sea life, including a snake eel (*Mixomyrophis pusillipinna*). Described from the island's waters in 1985, this eel is known to be endemic to the western Atlantic and is almost exclusively found around Anguilla. Unusually, its only other close relative, *M. longidorsalis*, is only found far away in the Red Sea, off the coast of Israel!

In a bid to protect the waters of Anguilla and its offshore islands, the government of the territory has created a number of marine reserves, including Dog Island, Island Harbour, Little Bay, Prickly Pear, Sandy Island, Seal Island and Shoal Bay. One reserve, Stoney Bay Marine Park, protects the wreck of a Spanish ship (*El Buen Consejo*) which ran aground on 8 July 1772 off Anguilla whilst on its way to Mexico with 50 Franciscan missionaries bound for the Philippines on board. A handful of more modern wrecks have been sunk off the coast to generate artificial reefs, including the *Meppel*, which was involved in the World War II battle at Dunkirk, the *Sarah*, which sank during Hurricane Klaus in 1984, and the Oosterdiep, which was sunk off the coast in 1990.

A native lobster (Photo: BCampbell65/Shutterstock.com).

A green turtle resting on a wreck (Photo: BCampbell65/Shutterstock.com).

A school of goatfish (Photo: BCampbell65/Shutterstock.com).

A green sea turtle swimming over sea-grass beds (Photo: Peter Richardson).

Population: 35 734 (2018)
Area: 417 sq. km of dry land
Currency: United States dollar
Capital: Cockburn Town (Grand Turk)
Flag: A Blue ensign bearing the islands' coat of arms—a conch, a cactus and a lobster.

TURKS AND CAICOS ISLANDS

The Turks and Caicos Islands lie 50 km southeast of the Bahamas. The Territory consists of two groups of islands, namely the Caicos Islands—which consist of nine main islands arranged in a fan—and the three Turks Islands. Both island groups are surrounded by many tiny islets and cays, but the Caicos Islands make up the majority of land in the territory by far. In total, the Turks and Caicos Islands comprise about 120 islands and cays, with a total combined area of 417 km². Far larger figures (about 615 sq. km) of total area are sometimes published, but these take into account vast, tidally flooded wetlands that constitute approximately 200 sq. km² of the territory.

The islands get their respective names from the 18th century English colloquialism for pirate, "Turk" (following two centuries of Ottoman piracy), as the islands were a centre of piracy during the 1700s, and a term in the language of the Lucayans (an indigenous Taíno tribe), *caya hico*, meaning 'string of islands'. Some suggest the Turks islands are named after the Turk's head cactus, as its red 'cephalium' resembles a fez, the traditional red hat of Turkey, but the modern fez only came into being after 1826, by which time the islands were long-since named.

The islands represent the highest points of a now submerged plateau that also includes southern Florida, the Bahamas and northern Cuba. Periods of geological uplift saw these coral reef encrusted points lifted above the water to give rise to the low-lying drifts of land that we see today. The Turks and Caicos Islands and the Bahamas collectively make up the Lucayan Archipelago, and are technically part of the West Indies and not the Caribbean, though they are often grouped with the Caribbean nations and the Caribbean UK Overseas Territories.

The first inhabitants of the Turks and Caicos Islands were the indigenous Taíno people, who arrived around AD 700 and spread across the Bahamas. These people called themselves the Lukka Kaya (people of the islands), giving rise to the name Lucaya used today. Their culture thrived on the islands into the 1400s, but swiftly ended with the arrival of Christopher Columbus. Spanish colonies established on islands close to the Turks and Caicos, frequently raided the Lucayans for slaves to work their mines and plantations in nearby colonies. These slaves were forced to perform hard labour and undergo conversion to Christianity. Resistance often resulted in death, though most slaves were simply worked into the grave under the extreme conditions. Within a matter of years, the Taíno had vanished, killed outright by the Spanish, by their forced labour or as a result of deadly diseases.

From the 1530s onwards, the Turks and Caicos Islands were uninhabited, becoming a stronghold of pirates including the legendary lady pirates Mary Read and Anne Bonny, along with Captain William Kidd and Edward Teach (Blackbeard). As piracy waned in the Caribbean in the middle of the 18th century, permanent settlement began and ownership of the islands was finally ceded to the English in 1764 after the Seven Years' War.

Turks and Caicos Islands

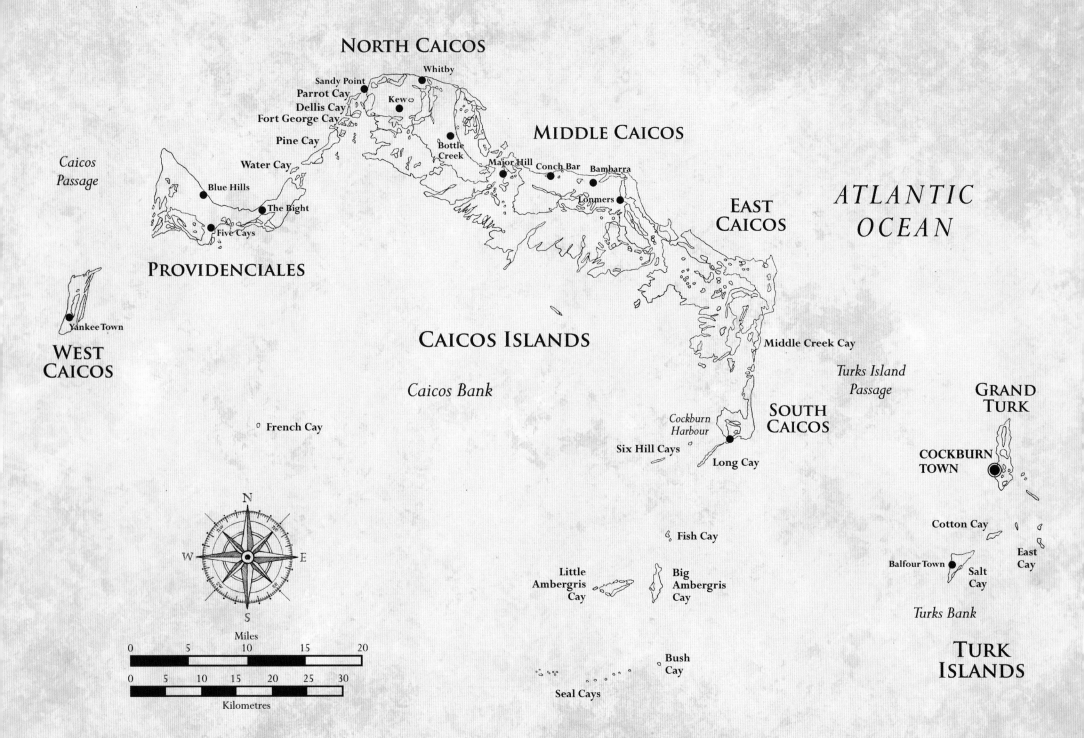

NORTH CAICOS

Whitby

Sandy Point
Parrot Cay
Dellis Cay
Fort George Cay

Kew

MIDDLE CAICOS

Pine Cay

Bottle Creek

Water Cay

Major Hill   Conch Bar   Bambarra

Caicos Passage

Blue Hills

EAST CAICOS

ATLANTIC OCEAN

The Bight

Lorimers

Five Cays

PROVIDENCIALES

CAICOS ISLANDS

Middle Creek Cay

Yankee Town

Turks Island Passage

WEST CAICOS

Caicos Bank

French Cay

SOUTH CAICOS

Cockburn Harbour

GRAND TURK

COCKBURN TOWN

Six Hill Cays

Long Cay

N

W   E

S

Cotton Cay

East Cay

Fish Cay

Balfour Town   Salt Cay

Little Ambergris Cay

Big Ambergris Cay

Turks Bank

Miles

0   5   10   15   20

Bush Cay

TURK ISLANDS

0   5   10   15   20   25   30

Kilometres

Seal Cays

Ruins of the Wade's Green plantation (Photo: Stewart McPherson).

Rock carvings made by captive slave workers (Photo: David M. Stone).

An illustration of slaves picking cotton.

Buildings in Cockburn Town (Photo: Stewart McPherson).

Cockburn Town

The settlement of Cockburn (pronounced *co-burn*) Town is situated on Grand Turk, the largest island in the Turks Islands group. Founded in 1681 as a temporary settlement by salt collectors, it has been the capital of the territory since 1766. During this period, the population swelled significantly as people flocked to the islands to profit from the highly lucrative salt trade, produced in natural lagoons modified into elaborate salt production pans. This production continued into the 20th century, ending in 1970 after a decade of collapse following the industrialised mining of salt elsewhere.

Modern Cockburn Town offers a glimpse of the past. The heart of the capital has changed little since the demise of the salt industry and several square kilometres of salt pans lie abandoned in the centre and the south of Grand Turk. The buildings of Cockburn Town's waterfront streets comprise rows of 19th century wooden warehouses and management buildings, many of which were constructed from timber salvaged from shipwrecks. Close to the wharfs, the buildings of shipwrights that designed and repaired the salt lighters can still be seen.

The ethnic make up of the Turks and Caicos reflects its historic role in salt production; nearly 90% of the population is of African origin, descendants of those brought here against their will by the slave trade as free labour.

A salt evaporation pond on Grand Turk (Photo: Nenad Basic/Shutterstock.com).

Raking Salt, Turks Islands, B. W.

Workers raking salt near Cockburn Town.

Landscape and Habitats

In geographical terms, the Turks and Caicos islands are contiguous with the Bahamas, being separated from the southeasternmost Bahamian islands by the Caicos Passage, which is 45 km wide at its narrowest point.

A vast 200 sq. km of the islands consist of tidal marshes and mangrove swamp, meaning that only two thirds of the territory are represented by permanently dry land. As coralline islands, the landscape is flat and soils generally poor, although they were originally covered by native forests. These forests survived until the late 1780s, when British loyalists fleeing North America during the American Revolution ordered their 1200 slaves to pull down the trees to make way for plantations of cotton, sugar cane and sisal.

The arable areas were productive for a relatively short period of a few decades only. The loss of the natural forest cover caused the thin soils of the islands to erode quickly and leach nutrients. After a few years of high yields, the output of the plantations declined dramatically and they suffered further from infestations by pests, falling cotton and sugar prices, as well as a series of severe hurricanes.

Today, the most pristine native forests are the mangroves and salt marshes, as those habitats were left untouched owing to their lack of perceived value. They are very important breeding and feeding locations for wildlife.

An aerial view of tidal marshes (Photo: Mike Pienkowski).

A native osprey watching for prey (Photo: Ramunas Bruzas/Shutterstock.com).

Mudjin Harbour, Middle Caicos (Photo: Stewart McPherson).

Salt Industry

Although salt was first collected on the islands in 1563, production of salt began when Bermudian salt collectors started to make seasonal visits to harvest this highly valued commodity, often called 'white gold'. The vast, shallow lagoons and dry summers ensured high productivity, and lent themselves to the eventual creation of complex systems of channels, sluices and evaporation pans; in an era when mechanised salt extraction was not possible, the islands' output of salt was immense. The dried sea salt was racked into large piles and transported to ships waiting offshore for sale to customers in North America, particularly Newfoundland, where it was used to salt and preserve cod. Salt farming was so lucrative that, in 1776, Bermudian salt merchants ignored British embargoes to sell salt to the revolutionary army of George Washington. During the 1780s, up to 1000 labourers and as many as 75 ships were sent from Bermuda to the salt islands to collect the precious resource! Now abandoned, the salt pans are a magnet for wildlife, particularly birds such as flamingoes, as well as herons and various wading species.

A reddish egret (*Egretta rufescens*) and a great egret (*Ardea alba*) fishing in a salt pan on Grand Turk (Photo: Mike Pienkowski).

The abandoned salt pans across the Turks and Caicos Islands are now refuges for American flamingos (*Phoenicopterus ruber*) and dozens of other bird species (Photo: Mike Pienkowski).

A male greater Antillean bullfinch (*Loxigilla violacea ofella*). This subspecies is endemic to Middle and East Caicos (Photo: Mike Pienkowski).

A thick-billed vireo (Vireo crassirostris stalagmium). This subspecies is endemic to the Turks and Caicos Islands (Photo: Mike Pienkowski).

Wildlife

The Turks and Caicos islands are home to an interesting array of wildlife. Although native mammals include bats, manatees and whales, there are no endemic species. Likewise, an astounding 224 species of birds have also been reported from across the archipelago; of those, none are endemic, and about half are infrequent visitors, but still leaving over 100 native birds that breed across the various types of habitat on the islands.

The abandoned salt pans that surround Cockburn Town are now conserved as historic sites, attracting vast numbers of shorebirds that wade through the pinkish, algae-rich brine in search of food. As the ponds extend into the heart of the town, they draw birds into central Cockburn and offer one of the best opportunities to view wild birds in an urban environment. Flocks of flamingos are commonly seen and are especially popular amongst tourists. Since the birds have become habituated to passing cars and pedestrians, they are exceptionally easy to view.

There are two bird subspecies that are endemic to the Turks and Caicos Islands, as well as one bird species that is restricted to the Territory and the adjacent Bahamas, and another that is restricted to the Turks and Caicos Islands and nearby Cuba. Countless waterbirds migrate to the islands during winter from North America and the Arctic, as do many songbirds.

A juvenile yellow-crowned night heron (*Nyctanassa violacea*) (Photo: Mike Pienkowski).

The tiny pygmy gecko (Photo: Stewart McPherson).

When it comes to reptiles, the islands excel, being home to an impressive number of endemic species. The ancestors of all land animals that live on the islands today reached the islands by travelling across the ocean. This process favoured reptiles due to their ability to survive long voyages without food or fresh water. There are seven endemic reptile species and two endemic subspecies on the small islands, some of which display unusual traits. The Turks Island rainbow boa (*Chilabothrus chrysogaster chrysogaster*) has iridescent scales, while the Turks and Caicos curly-tail lizard (*Leiocephallus psammodromus*) has a long, conspicuously curled tail which it flicks and twitches as a 'false head' to distract predators.

The Caicos Islands dwarf boa (*Tropidophis greenwayi*), which is not only unique to the Caicos Islands but has diversified within the Territory to form endemic subspecies on Ambergris Cay and South Caicos, has evolved into one of the smallest boa species in the world, maturing at a length of just 25 cm. The Turks Dwarf Gecko (*Sphaerodactylus underwoodi*) and the Caicos Dwarf Gecko (*Sphaerodactylus caicosensis*) are even more extreme, growing to just 5 cm in length and stalking prey amongst the leaf litter.

The unique Caicos barking gecko (*Aristeliger hechti*) was thought to be extinct for over 40 years until it was rediscovered in the early 2000s by the surveying UK Overseas Territories Conservation Forum.

The colouration of tiny endemic Caicos Dwarf Gecko (*Sphaerodactylus caicosensis*) may be very variable (Photo: Matthew L. Niemiller).

The Turks Islands rainbow boa (*Chilabothrus chrysogaster chrysogaster*) has iridescent scales (Photo: Matthew L. Niemiller).

Like so many other Caribbean islands, Turks and Caicos are home to a unique species of iguana; the population of Turks and Caicos rock iguanas (*Cyclura carinata*) was devastated by introduced predators such as cats, dogs and the ever-problematic black rat, mirroring the fate of the iguanas of the Cayman Islands, British Virgin Islands and other island chains. The species lost more than 95% of its original range and survives today on just a few isolated, uninhabited offshore cays.

In contrast with the iguana conservation initiatives on the Cayman Islands and the British Virgin Islands, the future of the Turks and Caicos rock iguana has been secured partly through the translocation of many of the last remaining specimens to islands that are free of predators. It is hoped that, with continued protection, viable populations will survive and procreate in these natural habitats.

One of the main refuge islands is Little Water Cay, which lies close to Providenciales, the most densely populated Caicos island. It now harbours a breeding population that consists of over 2000 iguanas. Tourists are allowed to visit the island and follow a custom-made board walk which is proving to be an increasingly popular attraction. Further iguana refuges have been successfully established on other small cays and it is hoped that the future of the species is now secure, if only across a tiny proportion of its former range.

A native rock iguana (Photo: Norman Rogers/Shutterstock.com).

Once warmed by the sun, the rock iguana can change colour to absorb less heat (Photo: BlueOrange Studio/Shutterstock.com).

An endemic *Encyclia* orchid (Photo: Stewart McPherson).

Flora

Although much of the native forests covering the islands were decimated during the plantation era, when slaves cleared the land to make way for agriculture, the islands remain home to a number of surviving endemic plants. These include the winter orchid (*Encyclia caicensis*), the ambergris buttonwood (*Spermacoce capillaris*), Britton's buttonbush (*S. brittonii*), Caroline's pink flower (*Stenandrium carolinae*), slender-stemmed peppergrass (*Lepidium filicaule*) and a relative of the oleander, *Metastelma stipitatum*.

Up to 10% of the islands were previously covered by forests of Caribbean pine (*Pinus caribaea* var. *bahamensis*), but in a tragedy that echoes the loss of native juniper forests on Bermuda, up to 95% of the forests were destroyed when, in 2001, scale insects (*Toumeyella parvicornis*) were accidentally introduced to the islands on Christmas trees imported from the mainland United States. With few if any native predators to keep their numbers in check, their numbers exploded; a plague of scale insects spread through the pine forests, covering the trees and draining them of sap. Also depositing sugary 'honey dew' onto their foliage, the trees were quickly covered in sooty mould that impeded their ability to photosynthesise and transpire effectively.

Recovery plans include the planting of scale resistant trees and long term storage of seed, but it is too early to know whether these plans will work.

The endemic Turks and Caicos heather (*Limonium bahamense*), the territory's national flower (Photo: Mike Pienkowski).

Pine forest killed by introduced scale insects (Photo: Stewart McPherson).

Marine Environment

The coral reefs of the Turks and Caicos Islands are some of the largest, most beautiful and biodiverse reefs in the entire Caribbean. Vast gardens of coral give way to extensive drop-offs that plunge to 2400 m. The combination of deep waters and the shallow banks provide an important breeding area for whales. Close to shore, there are many submerged cave systems; an enormous blue hole (a sink hole) lies on the shallow Caicos bank south of Middle Caicos. This feature, called the Ocean Hole, may be the widest blue hole in the world.

In the brackish and salty waters of the islands inland caves, at least ten species of weird and wonderful cave-dwelling invertebrates have been identified, including a 'remipede' crustacean (*Micropacter yagerae*), a member of an entirely endemic family which looks like an underwater centipede!

In addition to having waters rich with turtles, which are now helped to breed through heavily regulated fisheries that ban egg collection and disturbance of turtles during their breeding season, the islands are also home to the world's only conch farm. Set up in 1984 in response to the collapsing queen conch (*Lobatus gigas*) populations across the Caribbean, this facility on the island of Providenciales aims to supply the demand for conch meat without impacting further on wild populations. Of the 1.5 million conchs raised annually, 500 000 juveniles are returned to the wild each year!

A diving humpback whale (Photo: Yann Hubert/Shutterstock.com).

Reef fish exploring colourful corals (Photo: Joe Barbarite/Shutterstock.com).

An eagle ray (Photo: David M. Stone).

Coastal cliffs on the Akrotiri peninsula, Cyprus (Photo: Shutterstock.com).

Population: 18 000 (2018)
Area: 254 sq. km of dry land
Currency: Euro
Capital: Episkopi
Flag: The Union Flag of the United Kingdom—the crosses of St Andrew, St Patrick and St George.

AKROTIRI AND DHEKELIA

Akrotiri and Dhekelia, officially titled the Sovereign Base Areas of Akrotiri and Dhekelia, are two British military establishments on the island of Cyprus which remained under British jurisdiction when the 1960 Treaty of Establishment achieved independence for the Republic of Cyprus from the British Empire. Despite being separated by a distance of 70 km, the two areas together represent a single territory. Akrotiri is known as the Western Sovereign Base Area and measures 123 sq. km in size, whereas Dhekelia is the Eastern Sovereign Base Area and covers 131 sq. km.

The two Sovereign Base Areas are run by the Sovereign Base Area Administration. Each includes restricted-access military stations as well as areas that are completely open to the public. Unlike all of the other UK Overseas Territories, administration of the Sovereign Base Area is funded by, and reports to, the UK Ministry of Defence in London rather than the Foreign and Commonwealth Office. Uniquely, the territory does not have its own flag, is the only place under British sovereignty to use the Euro, and its laws are those of the Republic of Cyprus where practicable.

Being situated on Cyprus, Akrotiri and Dhekelia are at the eastern edge of the Mediterranean and close to the Middle East and Suez Canal. The two bases are thus of vital strategic significance to the United Kingdom. The areas have roles as staging posts for military aircraft and ground forces en route to the region. They also serve as important electronic intelligence gathering stations and remote monitoring outposts. Positioned just 45 minutes flying time from Iraq and Syria, the territory played a crucial role in enabling recent British military operations in the region, not least imposing no-fly zones over Saddam Hussein's regime and more recently attacking and intercepting terrorist targets of the so-called Islamic State.

Around 3500 military personnel of British Forces Cyprus are based at Akrotiri and Dhekelia, generally on three year rotations along with their partners and children (an additional 4500 people). A further 10000 citizens of the Republic of Cyprus also live and work in the two areas, mainly in villages that existed prior to 1960. The civilian residents are citizens of the Republic and do not have British Overseas Territories citizenship status, but they are permitted to live and work within the areas outside the restricted-access military stations. Both areas have open borders with the Republic of Cyprus, allowing many to live in the territory and travel to the Republic for work, or vice versa.

Under the terms of the Treaty of Establishment, the Sovereign Base Areas are specifically for military purposes, thus expansion of civilian development beyond pre-existing extents is largely prohibited.

Sovereign Base Areas

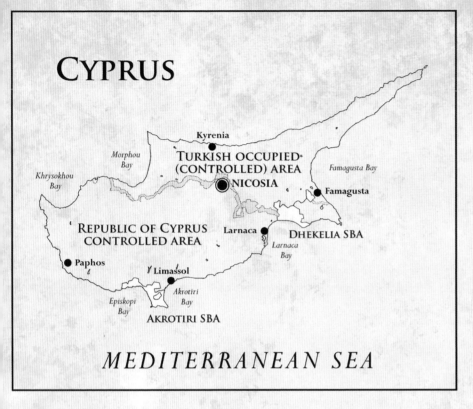

CYPRUS

Kyrenia

Morphou Bay

Khrysokhou Bay

TURKISH OCCUPIED (CONTROLLED) AREA

NICOSIA

Famagusta Bay

Famagusta

REPUBLIC OF CYPRUS CONTROLLED AREA

Larnaca

DHEKELIA SBA

Larnaca Bay

Paphos

Limassol

Episkopi Bay

Akrotiri Bay

AKROTIRI SBA

MEDITERRANEAN SEA

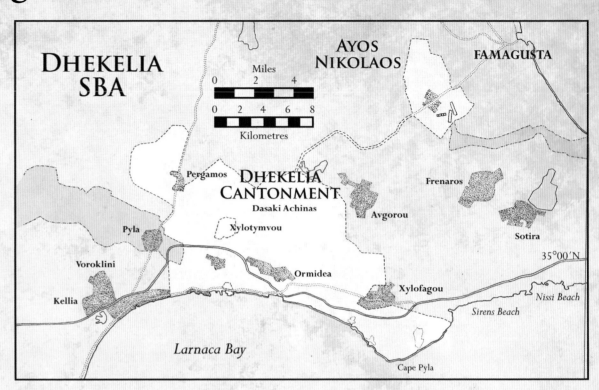

DHEKELIA SBA

AYOS NIKOLAOS

FAMAGUSTA

Miles
0   2   4

Kilometres
0   2   4   6   8

Pergamos

DHEKELIA CANTONMENT

Frenaros

Dasaki Achinas

Avgorou

Sotira

Pyla

Xylotymvou

Voroklini

Ormidea

Xylofagou

35°00′N

Kellia

Nissi Beach

Sirens Beach

Larnaca Bay

Cape Pyla

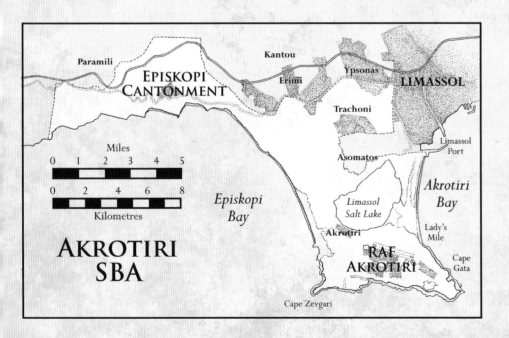

Paramili

Kantou

Ypsonas

LIMASSOL

EPISKOPI CANTONMENT

Erimi

Trachoni

Miles
0   1   2   3   4   5

Limassol Port

Kilometres
0   2   4   6   8

Asomatos

Episkopi Bay

Limassol Salt Lake

Akrotiri Bay

Akrotiri

Lady's Mile

AKROTIRI SBA

RAF AKROTIRI

Cape Gata

Cape Zevgari

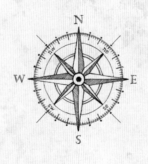

N

W   E

S

☐ Sovereign Base Areas

▨ De-militarised zone

Episkopi

The Headquarters of the Sovereign Base Areas are located in Episkopi. Episkopi is the home to the civilian and military administration headquarters and thus functions as the seat of government.

The region around Episkopi, but the Akrotiri Peninsula in particular, is home to over 100 mainly Greco-Roman ancient ruin sites, many dating back over 2500 years. The prohibition of development in the base areas has meant that these sites have been left remarkably intact.

In the same manner, the wildlife and landscape of the territory, which includes rare and sensitive wetlands, have also been safeguarded and offer important habitat for a wide range of plant and animal species.

Landscape and Habitats

Cyprus is a rocky and fairly mountainous island with a highly temperate Mediterranean climate, including a significant number of important habitat types, including some that are increasingly rare in the often highly developed Mediterranean region.

Akrotiri alone is home to 27 distinct habitat types, making it one of the most biologically diverse parts of Cyprus, including reed-filled marshes, salt lakes, dunes and juniper and pine forests.

The remains of a temple complex near Kourion beach (Photo: Stewart McPherson).

An ancient amphitheatre at Kourion (Photo: Stewart McPherson).

Native vegetation on the west coast of the Akrotiri peninsula, looking northwest towards the Episkopi Cantonment (Photo: Stewart McPherson).

Part of a vast flock of greater flamingo flying over the Akrotiri salt lake (Photo: Thomas Hadjikyriakou).

A greater flamingo (*Phoenicopterus roseus*) at the Akrotiri salt lake (Photo: Mike Pienkowski).

A wood sandpiper (*Tringa glareola*) visiting Akrotiri on its vast migration route (Photo: Mike Pienkowski).

A resident common kingfisher (*Alcedo atthis*) (Photo: Mike Pienkowski).

Wetlands are vital wildlife refuges worldwide (Photo: Mike Pienkowski).

Wildlife

The habitats of Akrotiri attract over 300 species of birds (70% of the bird species recorded from Cyprus so far). Without doubt the most important site of all is a vast, shallow salt lake in the middle of the peninsula which, like the adjacent smaller freshwater and salt marshes, is a magnet for wildlife. Virtually all of the salt lake is less than 1 m deep and often much shallower, especially during summer. This provides ideal conditions for brine shrimp, which in turn account for the presence of over 30 000 greater flamingos (*Phoenicopterus roseus*) which visit annually during winter. Several thousand flamingos may be present on the salt lake at any given time, although the greatest number recorded during a single day was over 17 000 in 2013.

Freshwater marshes and salt lakes are very rare in the Mediterranean, given its bedrock of porous limestone. The freshwater wetlands and salt lake of Akrotiri are used by millions of birds as a staging post for wider migrations, as well as for overwintering and breeding. The habitats surrounding the wetlands are also important habitats for two bird species which breed in Cyprus and nowhere else: the Cyprus warbler (*Sylvia melanothorax*) and the Cyprus pied wheatear (*Oenanthe cypriaca*). Accordingly, the wetland areas of Akrotiri are regarded as the most important wetland habitat for birds on Cyprus, and have been designated a Ramsar Wetland of International Importance.

A pair of feeding herons (Photo: Mike Pienkowski).

Remote cliffs offer habitat to rare birds (Photo: Vladislav Jirousek/Shutterstock.com).

The profusion of bird life across Akrotiri supports large numbers of birds of prey, particularly Eleanora's falcons (*Falco eleonorae*). Several carrion feeders are also present, including Cyprus' only breeding colony of griffon vultures (*Gyps fulvus*). This impressive bird can have a wing span of nearly 3 metres. Unfortunately, the Cypriot population collapsed over the 20th century and just sixteen birds are known to remain on the island today, of which eight nest on the cliffs near Episkopi. The small colony is persistent and around two chicks are successfully reared each year. It is hoped that the numbers will continue to build.

Unusually, Cyprus is the site of significant illegal bird trapping owing to its importance as a migration flyway for birds travelling between Africa and Europe. An estimated 2.4 million birds are trapped by mist nets and limesticks (perches of wood covered in a powerful adhesive). This damaging activity, which earns local crime gangs an estimated €15 million each year, is mainly carried out to supply local demand for a traditional dish called *ambelpoulia*, which consists of boiled, fried, grilled or pickled songbirds. Given the indiscriminate nature of the trapping methods used, many protected species are caught and killed by the trappers. While officially banned, an estimated 260 000 birds were illegally seized from the British administered zones in 2017.

A griffon vulture (Photo: Pantelis Charilaou).

The 3 metre wingspan of a griffon vulture (Photo: Pantelis Charilaou).

The vegetation that surrounds Akrotiri's salt lake is rich with smaller animal life. It is home to populations of the European chameleon (*Chamaeleo chamaeleon*). This species can grow up to 40 cm in length and, in common with larger and more well-known chameleons from Madagascar, it can change colour rapidly to camouflage itself, to communicate with other chameleons and to display warnings and moods.

The appearance of the European chameleon is variable across its range, but the Akrotiri population generally takes on mottled patterns of light brown, pale yellow, cream and green, although it may show darker colouration if threatened, angry or when mating.

The devil's flower mantis (*Blepharopsis mendica*) also thrives in Akrotiri's vegetation. This beautiful insect has fixed patterns of colour that can be remarkably similar to those of the European chameleon. All parts of the mantis's body may be mottled with green, white and brown patterns; it even competes with the chameleon for the same arthropod prey in the same habitat, however as a substantial insect, it may also inadvertently become the prey of stalking chameleons.

A number of reptiles are known from the territory, including many of the ten species of snake found on the island, as well as a number of skinks and a robust agamid lizard.

A devil's flower mantis (Photo: Pantelis Charilaou).

A green chameleon (Photo: Vladimir Martynovsky/Shutterstock.com).

Wildflowers on the Akrotiri coast (Photo: Vladislav Jirousek/ Shutterstock.com).

Flora

On the whole Cyprus is home to wide number of different plant, including over 100 endemic plants, many of which are native to the Troödos Mountains of central Cyprus, outside of the territory. Even so, the undeveloped nature of Akrotiri and Dhekelia and its varied habitats has ensured that many rare species find refuge within its confines. According to some estimates, 80–100% of the lowlands of the island were once covered in forest, but this has almost entirely been lost. The wildflower scrub that now predominates is the vegetation that survived after the removal of the trees by ancient civilisations, yet it is nevertheless important for native plants. As a result, the nature reserves of the territory, though not forest covered either, are some of the finest on the island for their intact modern ecosystems.

34 different orchid species are known from Akrotiri peninsula, amounting to two thirds of all those known from Cyprus. The most fascinating of all are the bee orchids (*Ophrys*), whose exquisite flowers mimic female solitary bees or wasps to trick males into pollinating them. The lip of the flower resembles an insect—complete with patches of hair and iridescence—and perhaps most importantly releases analogues of sex pheromone so potent that insect paramours will actively try to mate with foreign objects coated with them!

Kotschy's bee orchid (Photo: Pantelis Charilaou).

Marine Environment

The territory claims territorial waters of a mere 3 nautical miles, though the United Nations maintains that the territory reserves the right to claim up to 12 nautical miles.

Nevertheless, the beaches of Akrotiri are very important nesting sites for the endangered green turtle (*Chelonia mydas*) and the vulnerable loggerhead turtle (*Caretta caretta*).

Both turtle species are protected. The beaches within the Sovereign Base Area of Akrotiri, whilst not closed to bathers or tourism, are large, pristine and remote enough that they remain mostly free from people, allowing for very good turtle breeding colonies to develop. With little foot traffic, laying turtles are unlikely to be disturbed or their eggs inadvertently crushed, and so Akrotiri's beaches serve as important habitat for these vulnerable turtle species.

The waters off Cyprus are very clean given the island's isolated position in the Mediterranean, and ocean life is diverse, accounting for a health diving industry which makes use of a number of wrecks that sit close to the coastline. Diving within the territory mainly occurs in Dhekelia owing to the presence of nearby commercial diving operations, whereas Akrotiri is more remote and thus less often visited by divers.

An adult green turtle (Photo: blue-sea.cz/Shutterstock.com).

A hermit crab feeding at night (Photo: DAAgius/Shutterstock.com).

A venomous long spine urchin (Photo: f8grapher/Shutterstock.com).

The great Rock of Gibraltar stands as sentry over the territory (Photo: EmperorCosar/Shutterstock.com)

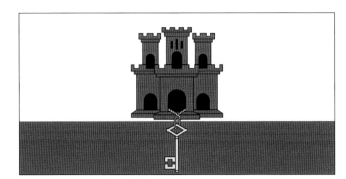

Population: 32 194 (2015)
Area: 6.7 sq. km of dry land
Currency: Gibraltar pound
Capital: Gibraltar
Flag: Banner of arms based on the coat of arms of Gibraltar—a castle and key representing the colony's sentinel position.

GIBRALTAR

Despite being the smallest of all the UK Overseas Territories, Gibraltar is without doubt the best known. Gibraltar is a peninsula, consisting of a narrow finger of land that extends from the southern end of the Spanish province of Cádiz, Andalusia, into the mouth of the Mediterranean. This flat, sandy isthmus extends for about a kilometre from the Iberian Peninsula before giving rise to 'the Rock', a dramatic, 426 m high fortress-like outcrop of Jurassic limestone 3.5 km long (north to south) and 1 km wide (east to west).

Gibraltar, which is home to the majority of Gibraltarians, is a densely populated city nestled at the foot of the western slopes of the Rock, partly on land reclaimed from the sea. The city sprawls across most of the western lowlands, but small villages of unique character are scattered in the south and on the eastern side, including Sandy Bay and Catalan Bay. A series of breakwaters and jetties have been constructed on the western side of Gibraltar to shelter a Royal Navy base and a major port facility that fronts the city.

The Rock of Gibraltar is one of the most beautiful and distinctive features of the Mediterranean. Its symbolism amongst people goes back to the start of the region's recorded history, and certainly extends further into prehistory. The Phoenicians, sailors from present-day Lebanon, were amongst the first people known to have attached symbolic significance to Gibraltar. Their presence in the western Mediterranean is recorded from the 8th Century BCE, from which point onwards they dominated the Strait of Gibraltar. They called Gibraltar *Calpe* (hollow stone) because of the more than 200 cave systems known from the Rock. In 711, leading the Moorish conquest of southern Spain, Tariq ibn Ziyad crossed the Strait with a predominantly Berber army and landed in the vicinity of Gibraltar. Some claim that the Rock was renamed *Jebel Tariq*, the Mount of Tariq, the subsequent corruption of which gave rise to the name 'Gibraltar'. However, Dr John Cortes, Gibraltar's Minister of Environment, has pointed out that *Jebel Taer* (bird mountain—a possible reference to the striking twice-yearly migration of soaring birds between Europe and Africa) is a better fit. Muslim rule of Gibraltar lasted a total of 710 years, finally ending in 1462. During this time considerable fortifications were built, many of which survive today.

In 1704, during the War of the Spanish Succession, a combined Anglo-Dutch fleet captured Gibraltar for the Hapsburg Archduke Charles of Austria. The invaders, led by the English majority, landed the next day and, not surprisingly, encountered little opposition. In 1713, in order to secure the withdrawal of Britain from the war, the Treaty of Utrecht was negotiated, with Spain ceding control of Gibraltar to Britain, Article X of the Treaty stating that the town of Gibraltar, its fortifications and port were ceded to the British Crown "for ever, without any exception or impediment whatsoever". Since that time, Gibraltar has withstood countless takeover sieges and even a large-scale offensive by the Nazis in World War II. To date, the Rock has never fallen out of British control.

Gibraltar

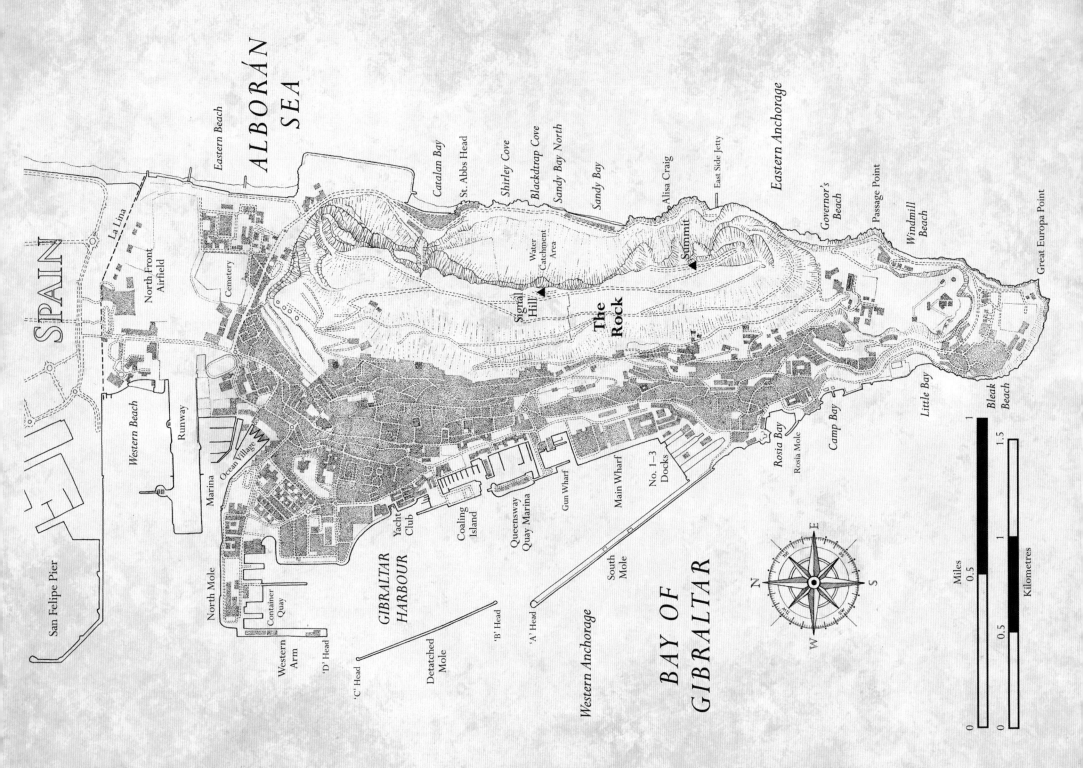

A depiction of Gibraltar as it may originally have appeared from the Spanish side of the Bay of Gibraltar (courtesy of the Gibraltar Museum).

The continual sieges faced by Gibraltar have directly affected the territory's defensive capabilities. Despite the treaties, several Spanish monarchs made unsuccessful attempts to regain the Rock, including numerous sieges that culminated in the Great Siege of Gibraltar from 1779–1783. The siege remains one of the longest continuous sieges in modern history. The besieged British strengthened fortifications across Gibraltar and carved tunnels through the Rock to poke cannons through the northern cliffs towards the isthmus with Spain, firing on the waves of attacking forces approaching from the mainland. With fewer than 7000 men and only 96 guns, the British prevailed against the 40 000 men and 246 guns of the Spanish and French.

When the territory was surrounded by enemy forces in World War II, Winston Churchill ordered the digging of a vast tunnel network in the rock, with over 52 km of tunnels being dug during the course of the war! The labyrinth within the Rock served to house tanks, planes, equipment and thousands of military personnel in the event that Gibraltar was invaded. Throughout the war, the military base at Gibraltar was given the name HMS *Cormorant*. It was a major airbase, with vast numbers of planes stationed on an airfield constructed along the isthmus between the Rock and Spain. In the end, the outpost proved to be essential for the movement of forces to North Africa and across the Mediterranean for the liberation of southern Europe.

Gibraltar's Moorish Castle (Photo: Toni Genes/Shutterstock.com).

Defenses in St George's Hall, inside the Rock (Photo: Marzolino/Shutterstock.com).

Aircraft stationed at HMS Cormorant during the World War II (Imperial War Museum).

Gibraltar

Gibraltar functions as a non-sovereign city state, thus Gibraltar is also its own capital, operating with almost complete internal democratic self-government through an elected parliament. The 32 000 or so Gibraltarians are all British Citizens, however they have a culture and language all of their own. Sometimes referred to as *llanitos* (possible 'people of the flatlands'), the Gibraltarians speak *llanito* (pron. *yaneeto*)—alongside the official language, English, and the widespread Andalusian dialect of Spanish—a language consisting of Spanish heavily influenced by British English, but also other languages such as medieval Genoese, Maltese and even a mostly extinct Judeo-Spanish language called Haketia! Speakers of llanito frequently code switch, that is, jump from Spanish to English as the subject matter demands.

Gibraltar has long been given the right of self-determination by the British. With claims to the territory renewed by Spain's dictator General Franco in the 1950s, Gibraltarians voted overwhelmingly to remain under British sovereignty in the Gibraltar sovereignty referendum of 1967; and again in 2002, 98% of Gibraltarians rejected a remarkable compromise proposal of shared sovereignty on which Spain and Britain were both said to have reached broad agreement. Since that time, the British Government has committed to respecting the wishes of Gibraltarians.

Searchlights pierce the night sky during an air-raid practice on Gibraltar, 20 November 1942 (War Office official photographer Dallinson G W (Lieut.)/Imperial War Museum).

A view looking down onto the City of Gibraltar from the upper slopes of the Rock (Photo: Stewart McPherson).

Landscape and Habitats

The Gibraltar peninsula is dominated by the limestone promontory known as the Rock. In ancient times, it was known as one of the Pillars of Hercules. The Rock is 'monolithic', meaning the entire feature consists of a single giant piece of rock. Although the material that makes up the rock is about 175–200 million years old, the processes that lifted it up into its current position occurred about 5 million years ago when the African and Eurasian tectonic plates collided. The violence of this process is reflected in the rock itself: the oldest material is found on top of the Rock, while the youngest makes up its base, meaning the entire thing was turned upside down as it was pushed upwards!

The Rock is connected to the Spanish mainland by a 'tombolo', essentially a spit of land that arose from the accumulation of sand. This flat area of land is a mere 3 metres above sea level, in contrast to the rock itself. The sides of the Rock are steep or vertical on the north and eastern sides and more gradually sloping to the south and west. Narrow coastal lowlands surround the Rock on all sides and expand into a series of stony terraces to the south. The poor limestone soils support a remarkably rich Mediterranean scrub with a significant wildflower and invertebrate community, which in turn support millions of birds migrating between Africa and Europe annually.

Wildflower meadows cover the eastern side of the Rock across the Great Gibraltar Sand Dune. These support populations of arthropods and reptiles, all of which contribute to Gibraltar's rich ecosystem (Photo: Leslie Linares BEM BEd ARPS).

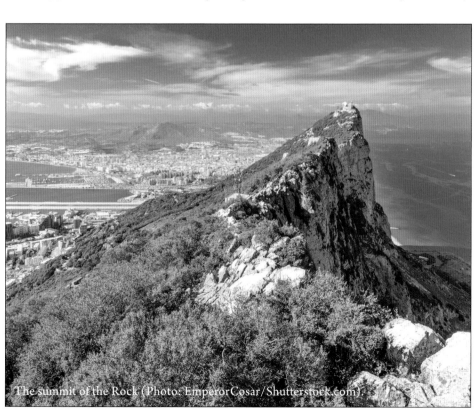

The summit of the Rock (Photo: EmperorCosar/Shutterstock.com).

A view of the Gibraltar Peninsula from the southeast, looking northwest. (Photo: Stewart McPherson).

A family of Barbary macaques (Photo: Edwin Butter/Shutterstock.com).

The Barbary macaques of the Rock (Photo: Jon Slayer).

A baby Barbary macaque (Photo: Jon Slayer).

A curious teen (Photo: Timothy Knox/Shutterstock.com).

Gibraltar's Primates

The upper slopes of the Rock are known across the world as the home of the Barbary macaque (*Macaca sylvanus*). Gibraltar's macaque population is the only wild primate population in Europe. The origins of Gibraltar's macaques are uncertain. Beyond Gibraltar, Barbary macaques are naturally found in the mountains of Algeria and Morocco. In the past, this species was distributed across Europe as far north as the British Isles. Some believe the population on Gibraltar is a relict colony that has survived from ancient times, while others suggest that the species reached Gibraltar during times of lower sea levels. However, most authorities now believe that the Barbary macaques were introduced to the Rock by visitors, as the Phoenician, Carthaginian, Roman and Muslim inhabitants of Gibraltar all kept monkeys as novelty pets.

The macaques have a special significance to Gibraltar like no other animal. According to a local legend of the Great Siege, generally believed to be true, the then Governor George Augustus Eliott assumed that the 200 m tall cliffs of the Rock presented too formidable a barrier for enemy forces to attempt cross; he consequently stationed few British troops or lookouts along the Rock's high western cliffs. Noticing this vulnerability, Spain and France launched an ambitious attack that aimed to take the Rock by surprise. An assault team would climb over the Rock while the British positions were pounded by cannons from the Spanish lines and ships in the bay, descend onto the British and sweep through their positions. The assaulting force succeeded in climbing the Rock and began their surprise descent in the dead of night, but the party disturbed the macaques which screeched and screamed. A young drummer boy hearing the terrible noise quickly alerted the British garrison. The enemy was quickly found—200 were killed and 300 captured. The macaques were seen as saviours of the city: their thwarting of the attack led the Governor to prohibit the killing or mistreatment of the monkeys.

Gibraltar's significance as a hotspot for wild primates has taken on unexpected importance during the last few decades through a series of incredible discoveries. Neanderthal skulls have been unearthed in Gibraltar 9 times since 1848, and several of Gibraltar's Caves show clear signs of occupation by Neanderthals. Until the 1990s, it was widely believed that Neanderthals became extinct throughout their range across Europe and Asia around 35 000 years ago. However, in 2006 radiocarbon dating performed on artefacts from a number of Gibraltar's caves suggested that Neanderthals lived there as recently as 24 000 years before the present. This made Gibraltar the last stronghold for Neanderthals at a time when all other Neanderthals had already become extinct everywhere else for thousands of years!

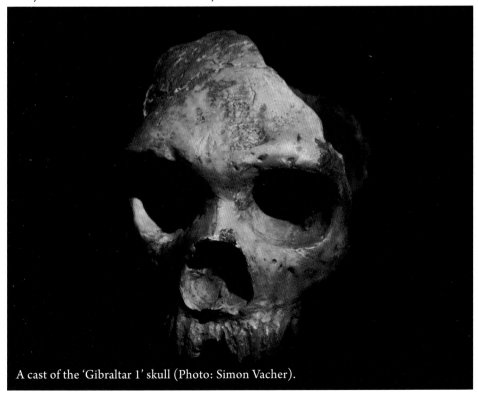

A cast of the 'Gibraltar 1' skull (Photo: Simon Vacher).

Entering Gorham's Cave (Photo: Stewart McPherson).

Some native beetles (Photo: Keith Bensusan).

Other Wildlife

Despite its size, Gibraltar is home to an impressive array of native wildlife. Mediterranean scrub and patches of woodland cover the sweeping, western slopes of Gibraltar's rocky outcrop, while the peninsula's coasts are home to extensive cave systems and rocky shorelines that provide important habitats for a plethora of species. These include the greater white-toothed shrew, common rabbit and seven species of bats, not to mention an array of native reptiles, including 2 species of geckos, 2 skinks, 2 lizards, 1 worm lizard and 7 snakes.

The large number of wildflowers across Gibraltar supports a complex ecosystem of invertebrates that includes over 700 species of beetles, 52 species of ants, over 500 species of butterflies and moths, as well as native stick insects and mantids. Discoveries of new arthropods continue to be made, which is remarkable considering the land area involved.

The unique vegetation, the abundance of flowers and the profusion of invertebrate life acts as the foundation that supports the 315 species of birds recorded from Gibraltar so far. Millions of birds migrate from Europe to warmer climes in Africa for the winter. However, soaring birds, such as birds of prey, need to limit their passage to the narrowest crossings and most of those breeding in western Europe travel to and from Africa via Gibraltar,

An exquisitely coloured cuckoo wasp (Photo: Gilbert Gonzalez).

A Burnet moth (Photo: Katherine Bennett uk/Shutterstock.com).

since the Strait represents the narrowest stretch of water between the two continents.

The greatest number of bird migrations takes place during March to May and August to October, at which times tens of thousands of birds may fly over the Rock daily. For this reason, Gibraltar has gained a reputation as the bird crossroads of Europe. Indeed, it is regarded as one of the best bird-watching sites on the entire continent.

Resident birds of prey include peregrine falcons, kestrels, lesser kestrels and little owls, as well as a single pair of eagle owls. Many birds of prey are declining across the Mediterranean region, which makes the populations in Gibraltar all the more significant. Gibraltar's peregrine falcon population is one of the densest in the world, with seven pairs known to breed on the cliffs of the Rock. Many large birds were extirpated from Gibraltar during the 19th and 20th centuries, but some are now returning; the rare eagle owl successfully nested on the Rock in 2005 after an absence of 100 years!

A Raptor Rehabilitation Unit has also been set up to ensure the well being of sick or injured birds. To date, nearly one thousand birds have been rehabilitated, including griffon vultures, peregrine falcons, lesser kestrels, buzzards, kites, sparrow hawks and harriers, along with a variety of other types of birds.

A rehabilitated peregrine falcon (Photo: Stewart McPherson).

A Barbary partridge (Photo: Andrew Dobson).

Flora

Over 650 different species of flowering plants grow in Gibraltar, of which over 270 are native. The vegetation of Gibraltar is specialised to survive hot, dry summer conditions and cooler, wet winters. Most of the Rock is dominated by tall, shrubby bushes that include wild olive (*Olea europaea*), buckthorn (*Rhamnus alaternus*), a pistachio shrub (*Pistacia lentiscus*), Osyris (*Osyris lanceolata*) and mainland Europe's only native palm species, the dwarf fan palm (*Chamaerops humilis*). The Rock is also the only place in Europe where the Gibraltar candytuft (*Iberis gibraltarica*) and the Gibraltar Thyme (*Thymus willdenowii*) grow in the wild outside of their native North Africa.

Remarkably, Gibraltar does have an endemic plant; the Gibraltar Campion (*Silene tomentosa*) is found there and nowhere else, thus its survival hinges on existing populations and cultivation of reservoir plants by botanical gardens. The Gibraltar Sea Lavender (*Limonium emarginatum*) is endemic to the Strait of Gibraltar, being found on the Rock, the Tarifa area and along the African coast from Ceuta to Tangier.

The occurrence of unique plants on Gibraltar is partly due to its limestone bedrock and alkaline soils, which differ from the acidic sandstone of the immediate Spanish mainland. Gibraltar has a unique vegetation with African influences unlike any part of the nearby Iberian Peninsula.

The Gibraltar Candytuft (*Iberis gibraltarica*) (Photo: Leslie Linares BEM BEd ARPS).

The endemic Gibraltar Campion (*Silene tomentosa*) (Photo: Leslie Linares BEM BEd ARPS).

The non-endemic, but beautiful *Colchicum lusitanum* (Photo: Stewart McPherson).

Marine Environment

The waters around Gibraltar support extensive reefs with 300 species of fish, ten species of coral and one of the highest diversities of nudibranchs (sea-slugs) in the region. 54.87 sq. km of the Territory's waters are permanently conserved as the Southern Waters of Gibraltar Marine Special Protected Area, which serves as an important sanctuary for shoals of sardines and anchovies. The waters are also visited by numerous species of dolphins—especially bottlenose, striped and common dolphins—as well as many whales, including minke, sperm and fin whales, as well as orcas. The critically endangered Mediterranean monk seal (*Monachus monachus*) has occasionally been recorded.

One of the most threatened of all of Gibraltar's inhabitants is the Mediterranean ribbed limpet (*Patella ferruginea*). Sadly, this large, edible limpet species has suffered from intensive hunting by humans and suffered from pollution and development. Despite being a humble creature with little appeal to the average person, the Government of Gibraltar has gone to great lengths to ensure the well being of surviving limpet populations. In one case, a new development was halted until the local limpet population could be successfully moved to a new site, requiring the wholesale transfer of their large resident boulders to identical locations with optimal living conditions!

A pair of dolphins (Photo: Pepe Ramirez/Shutterstock.com).

A pod of long-finned pilot whales (Photo: Andrew Sutton/Shutterstock.com).

The Mediterranean ribbed limpet (*Patella ferruginea*) (Photo: H.M. Government of Gibraltar, Department of the Environment and Climate Change).

CONSERVATION LESSONS

Many of the UK Overseas Territories are like miniature versions of other parts of the world, and many of the conservation lessons that can be learned from the territories could be applied to situations elsewhere. For example, the removal of invasive pest species like rodents from South Georgia or from delicate bird habitats off Bermuda apply as much to the mainlands and islands of Australia and New Zealand—both of which have suffered extreme losses of endemic species diversity as a result of competition and predation from introduced species—albeit on wholly different scales.

Although many of the UK Overseas Territories are minuscule pin-pricks of land, they are of disproportionate importance and often of regional or even global significance for a number of reasons:

- They represent the only home of more than one thousand unique plant and animal species.
- They provide vital sites for various annual events—such as breeding or feeding—in the life of migratory animals, whose journeys may span entire hemispheres.
- Many support pristine or near pristine examples of various types of ecosystem, some of which are the most intact examples of their kind to survive anywhere on Earth.

Some of the UK Overseas Territories have actually led the world in terms of conservation theory and action. For example, the territories are home to the earliest conservation legislation—such as the protections that were put in place for the cahows on Bermuda—and many adopted very early measures specifically intended to protect and conserve particular species or ecosystems—including the green turtles on Ascension Island, the Barbary macaques on Gibraltar and coral reefs across the British Indian Ocean Territory.

A male magnificent frigatebird (Photo: Don Mammoser/Shutterstock.com).

Terns swoop over the waters of Ascension (Photo: Kwest/Shutterstock.com).

The reasons for these examples of early and proactive conservation endeavours are varied. The small size and geographic isolation of many of the territories has left their wildlife particularly vulnerable to external factors—including invasion by introduced species and man-made changes to the environment—while the decline of certain species has been faster and certainly more noticeable than it can be on larger landmasses, as with the warrah (Falkland Islands wolf) on the Falkland Islands.

The human populations of many of the more remote territories have needed to be self-sufficient due to their isolation, so the fragility of local ecosystems came to be appreciated earlier and were the subject of greater concern than elsewhere. The depletion of local wildlife stocks such as seabirds or eggs can have dire consequences in places where they are amongst the only resources upon which people can survive; such an existence is already precarious, but introduce indiscriminate species like the black rat or mice and sustainable use becomes impossible as the finite resources are rapidly depleted if not entirely wiped out. Conservation has therefore in many cases been driven by necessity across many of the territories, only later being recognised as a key barrier dividing the survival of a species from its extinction.

The determined activities of conservationists across the UK Overseas Territories have given rise to hundreds of different projects that are being undertaken in an effort to slow, halt and in many cases reverse the decline of endemic species. In fact, only some of these efforts have been documented in this book such is the broad range of projects now running across the territories. Among the different approaches and initiatives that have been adopted, the following goals have been deemed to be amongst the most important:

- conserving the last fragments of native ecosystems;
- reversing damage through removal of non-native species to allow native ecosystems to regenerate;
- *ex-situ* conservation to preserve species where habitat is too degraded;
- careful future planning for development; and
- reducing negative population pressures such as hunting and fishing.

Conservation efforts across the UK Overseas Territories compare favourably with the rest of the world. These efforts are all the more impressive considering that the territories receive less than 1% of the UK's conservation funding, despite having at least 20 times the diversity of globally important animal and plant species found in the UK itself. Despite this funding disparity, globally significant conservation victories are being secured across the Territories, especially in terms of habitat recovery and conservation.

King penguins on the Falkland Islands (Photo: Roger Clark ARPS/Shutterstock.com).

More Information

If you have enjoyed reading about the wildlife, cultures, people and history of the UK Overseas Territories, please consider becoming a member of Friends of the British Overseas Territories (FOTBOT)— see **www.fotbot.org** for more information.

Friends of the British Overseas Territories is a charitable organisation (registered charity number 1156763) which works to increase awareness and promote understanding of the Overseas Territories, both in the UK and across the world. FOTBOT engages in a wide range of educational activities to raise public understanding about the conservation, protection and improvement of the physical and natural environments of the Territories, as well as of their history and geography. FOTBOT's activities and engagements are particularly focused on the education of young people aged 18–25, and educational visits to the Overseas Territories are frequently organised to offer interested individuals the opportunity to visit these fascinating places and witness their incredible cultures, wildlife, landscapes and history first hand.

FOTBOT works to promote understanding of the UK Overseas Territories (Photo: FOTBOT).

Membership of Friends of the British Overseas Territories offers many unique benefits, including invitations to regular membership-only events and information evenings that frequently feature high-profile speakers, as well as subscription to the FOTBOT Newsletter, a bespoke membership card and pin badge.

If you would like to learn more about the wildlife of the UK Overseas Territories and the conservation work that is taking place, please visit the website of the UK Overseas Territories Conservation Forum: **www.ukotcf.org.uk**

UKOTCF is devoted solely to conserving wildlife across the Territories. It is a UK-based charity with a small but dedicated team that has brought together a federation of on-the-ground conservation organisations in the Territories, as well as key supporting conservation bodies and specialists in Britain. Please consider supporting this important work by becoming a Friend of the UKOTs. You can learn more about this via their website.

Finally, the Britain's Treasure Islands website (**www.BritainsTreasureIslands.com**) is an online educational resource that supports the important work of the UK Overseas Territories Conservation Forum and many other conservation organisations. It includes overviews of each Territory, additional images, information on the Britain's Treasure Islands TV documentary series, as well as 42 mini-documentaries, all of which can be viewed free of charge online.

GLOSSARY

aquatic: (plant or animal) residing in a water habitat.

British Dependency: an outdated (and no longer used) term for the former British colonies that elected to remain under UK sovereignty. This term was in use after the passing of the British Nationality Act of 1981 until the British Overseas Territories Act of 2002.

British Overseas Territory: a synonym for 'UK Overseas Territory'.

colony: a country or area under the full or partial political control of another country.

crown dependencies: independently administered jurisdictions within UK sovereign territory that are not part of the United Kingdom or UK Overseas Territories but have some similarities to the latter. They are self-governing possessions of the Crown (defined uniquely in each jurisdiction).

country: a nation with its own government, occupying a particular territory.

dependency: a country or province controlled by another country or state.

empire: an extensive group of states or countries ruled over ultimately by a single authority.

endemic: (plant or animal) restricted to a certain place. The extent of 'the place' in question may range from an isolated lake to an area of forest or other ecosystem, a whole island, several islands within a biogeographical group, or a bigger geographical region, such as the Caribbean.

epiphytic: any plant that grows on another plant.

indigenous: (of a plant or animal) originating or occurring naturally in a particular place.

Foreign and Commonwealth Office: (commonly called the Foreign Office or FCO) is the department of the Government of the United Kingdom that is responsible for protecting and promoting British interests worldwide. The Foreign Office is also responsible for all but one of the UK Overseas Territories—the exception is the Territory of the Cyprus Sovereign Base Areas (Akrotiri and Dhekelia), which is the responsibility of the Ministry of Defence.

lithophyte: any plant that grows on or lives attached to rocks, also occasionally known as epilithic.

nation: a body of people (in many cases united by common descent, history, culture, or language) inhabiting a particular state or territory.

native: (plant or animal) originating or occurring naturally in a particular place.

non-native: (plant or animal) a species originating from elsewhere, introduced into an ecosystem either by accident or on purpose. May also be referred to in some circumstances as an 'alien' species

pelagic: (marine life or birds) relating to the open sea.

RAF: acronym for the Royal Air Force.

sovereignty: supreme power or authority (in a political context, the authority of a state to govern itself or another political entity).

species: a taxonomic unit of classification that defines a group of organisms that have one or more unifying characteristics separating them from any other group. Classically, species were defined as populations of organisms capable of interbreeding and producing fertile offspring, but this definition is not suited to plants as different species can often cross and produce fertile offspring.

state: a nation or territory considered as an organised political community under one government.

subspecies: a subdivision of a species, usually of interbreeding individuals geographically restricted and characterised by one or more distinct morphological features from other subspecies within the same species.

taxon (plural taxa): a taxonomic group of any rank, such as a species.

terrestrial: (plant or animal) residing on land.

territory: an area of land (and sometimes sea).

UKOT: acronym for UK Overseas Territory.

UK Overseas Territory: a territory under the jurisdiction and sovereignty of the United Kingdom.

ABOUT THE AUTHOR

Stewart McPherson is a British naturalist, author and film-maker. Fascinated by wildlife from an early age, he began writing his first book at the age of sixteen. Stewart went on to study geography at the University of Durham, and on graduating, he spent ten years climbing 300 mountains across the world (some of which were previously unexplored) to study and photograph carnivorous plants in the wild, to write a series of 25 books. Along the way, he co-discovered and co-named 35 new species/varieties of carnivorous plants, including some of the largest pitcher plants ever discovered.

After featuring in short sequences in several broadcast documentaries, Stewart and a camera team travelled to all of the UK Overseas Territories to document the wildlife, cultures, history and landscapes that the territories harbour. This journey took three years to complete, and the resulting documentary series was released as *Britain's Treasure Islands* on the BBC, National Geographic, SBS and many other channels. The accompanying *Britain's Treasure Islands* book was distributed across the UK, and (thanks to sponsorship by Lord Michael Ashcroft) copies were donated to all 5,350 secondary schools across the UK. Sponsorship from the Don Hanson Charitable Foundation and Friends of the British Overseas Territories enabled further copies to be donated to 2,000 public libraries and university libraries across the UK and the Overseas Territories.

RECOMMENDED READING

Andrew, T., 2007. *Field guide to the animals and plants of Tristan da Cunha and Gough Island.* Pisces Publications.

Clegg, P., 2009. *Governing the UK Caribbean overseas territories: A two-way perspective. Governance in the non-independent Caribbean*, pp.3-23.

George, B., *Establishing a National Trust in St Helena.*

Fogle, B., 2003. *The Teatime Islands.* Penguin.

Gell, F. and Watson, M., 2000. *UK Overseas Territories in the Northeast Caribbean: Anguilla, British Virgin Islands, Montserrat. Sea at the Millennium: an Environmental Evaluation*, pp.615-626.

Hamilton, M., 2006, October. *Turks and Caicos Islands invasive pine scale. In Biodiversity that matters: a conference on conservation in UK Overseas Territories and other small island communities* (Vol. 6, p. 12).

Hilton, G.M. and Cuthbert, R.J., 2010. *The catastrophic impact of invasive mammalian predators on birds of the UK Overseas Territories: a review and synthesis.* Ibis, 152(3), pp.443-458.

Hintjens, H. and Hodge, D., 2012. *The UK Caribbean Overseas Territories: governing unruliness amidst the extra-territorial EU.* Commonwealth & Comparative Politics, 50(2), pp.190-225.

McPherson, S., 2016. *Britain's Treasure Islands: A Journey to the UK Overseas Territories.* Redfern Natural History Productions.

Oldfield, S., 1987. *Fragments of paradise. A guide for conservation action in the UK Dependent Territories. Fragments of paradise. A guide for conservation action in the UK Dependent Territories.*

Pienkowski, M., 2010. *Wildlife in the UK Overseas Territories. Silent summer: The state of wildlife in Britain and Ireland*, pp.184-215.

Procter, D. and Fleming, L.V. eds., 1999. *Biodiversity: the UK Overseas Territories* (p. 131). Peterborough: Joint Nature Conservation Committee.

Ritchie, H., 1997. *The Last Pink Bits.* Army Quarterly & Defence Journal, 127(3), p.378.

Skinner, J., 2002. *British constructions with constitutions: the formal and informal nature of 'island' relations on Montserrat and Gibraltar.* Social Identities, 8(2), pp.301-320.

Winchester, S., 2009. *Outposts: Journeys to the Surviving Relics of the British Empire.* Harper Collins.

Index

A view across the rugged coast of Saint Helena (Photo: Shutterstock.com / Umomos).